T0311334

"This is a well-written, engaging overview of contemporary epistemology with a significant discussion of types of skepticism. An excellent option for an introductory level course, whether as a part of a larger introduction to philosophy or as an intro text to epistemology."

Ted Poston, *University of Alabama*

SKEPTICISM
THE BASICS

This book introduces students and other interested readers to the philosophical study of skepticism, a central and long-standing subject in philosophy. The first three chapters cover *knowledge*, providing the necessary foundation for introducing *skepticism* in the book's final three chapters. Throughout, the volume addresses basic questions in these two areas, such as:

- What are the differences between the three types of knowledge: direct knowledge, knowledge by ability, and propositional knowledge?
- What is the Gettier problem and why does it resist easy solutions?
- Why do philosophers still talk about René Descartes' techniques for raising doubts about what we can know but have largely forgotten Descartes' attempts to answer these doubts?
- How do we know that we're not just brains in a vat?
- Is Pyrrhonian skepticism—the idea that we know absolutely nothing—ultimately self-refuting?

With a glossary of key terms and suggestions for further reading, *Skepticism: The Basics* is an ideal starting point for anyone seeking a lively and accessible foray into the study of epistemology.

Juan Comesaña is Professor of Philosophy at the University of Arizona. He has published in epistemology and related areas, including *Being Rational and Being Right* (2020).

Manuel Comesaña is Professor of Philosophy and Doctor of Philosophy and has been a professor at the National University of Mar del Plata in Argentina for the last thirty years. He has published articles in philosophy journals and book chapters, as well as the book *Reason, Truth and Experience: An Analysis of Their Links in Contemporary Philosophy of Science, with Special Emphasis on Popper* (1996).

The Basics

The Basics is a highly successful series of accessible guidebooks which provide an overview of the fundamental principles of a subject area in a jargon-free and undaunting format.

Intended for students approaching a subject for the first time, the books both introduce the essentials of a subject and provide an ideal springboard for further study. With over 50 titles spanning subjects from artificial intelligence (AI) to women's studies, *The Basics* are an ideal starting point for students seeking to understand a subject area. Each text comes with recommendations for further study and gradually introduces the complexities and nuances within a subject.

Select philosophy titles in the series:

BIOETHICS (SECOND EDITION)
ALASTAIR V. CAMPBELL

EASTERN PHILOSOPHY (SECOND EDITION)
VICTORIA S. HARRISON

METAPHYSICS
MICHAEL REA

PHILOSOPHY (FIFTH EDITION)
NIGEL WARBURTON

SKEPTICISM: THE BASICS
JUAN COMESAÑA AND MANUEL COMESAÑA

For a full list of titles in this series, please visit www.routledge.com/The-Basics/book-series/B

SKEPTICISM

THE BASICS

Juan Comesaña and Manuel Comesaña

Routledge
Taylor & Francis Group

NEW YORK AND LONDON

Cover image: © Getty Images

First published 2022
by Routledge
605 Third Avenue, New York, NY 10158

and by Routledge
4 Park Square, Milton Park, Abingdon, Oxon, OX14 4RN

Routledge is an imprint of the Taylor & Francis Group, an informa business

© 2022 Taylor & Francis

The right of Juan Comesaña and Manuel Comesaña to be identified as authors of this work has been asserted in accordance with sections 77 and 78 of the Copyright, Designs and Patents Act 1988.

All rights reserved. No part of this book may be reprinted or reproduced or utilised in any form or by any electronic, mechanical, or other means, now known or hereafter invented, including photocopying and recording, or in any information storage or retrieval system, without permission in writing from the publishers.

Trademark notice: Product or corporate names may be trademarks or registered trademarks, and are used only for identification and explanation without intent to infringe.

Library of Congress Cataloging-in-Publication Data
A catalog record for this book has been requested

ISBN: 978-1-032-07710-9 (hbk)
ISBN: 978-1-032-07709-3 (pbk)
ISBN: 978-1-003-20844-0 (ebk)

DOI: 10.4324/9781003208440

Typeset in Bembo
by Apex CoVantage, LLC

CONTENTS

ACKNOWLEDGMENTS

We wish to thank those who read and made very valuable comments on previous drafts of this book: Richard Fumerton and Ted Poston (the once-anonymous reviewers for Routledge), Carolina Sartorio, and the students in our classes. The figures in Chapter 6 are courtesy of Ben Lawrence, and are based on sketches by Lewis Powell, themselves based on sketches by James Van Cleve. Many thanks as well to Andy Beck for his help with every aspect of this project.

INTRODUCTION

What do you know? "Not much," say the skeptics. Some skeptics even say, "Nothing at all." Are they right?

Perhaps a more important question is: does it matter whether they are right? We think it does. Some amount of skepticism is healthy and part of common sense. Neither of us, for instance, knows how many days it rained in what is now Tucson (Arizona) in the year 299 BC. It might even be healthy to cultivate a skeptical attitude with respect to many of the things we hear or read—not to dismiss them outright, but to subject them to appropriate levels of scrutiny. What is an appropriate level of scrutiny will vary from case to case, of course. If our friend tells us that it is raining outside, we believe him without engaging in any sort of sophisticated check on what he is saying. If the used car salesman tells us that this 1991 Chevy Cavalier is in perfect condition and has only "highway miles," we do not trust him immediately. These are easy cases.

So we have now clear cases where apparently skepticism is warranted (about how many days it rained in Tucson in 299 BC, for instance) and others where apparently we can very easily obtain knowledge (by trusting our friend when he tells us that it is raining outside, for instance). But there are also intermediate cases. We are writing this days before the 2020 presidential election in the United States. The polls indicate that Joe Biden has enough of a lead to win the election. But the polls also indicated that Hillary Clinton had enough of a lead over Donald Trump in 2016, and she lost the election. Is that enough to justify a skeptical attitude with respect to who will win the election? Maybe. But the pollsters, some observers say, learned their lesson, and they recalibrated their

DOI: 10.4324/9781003208440-1

polls to consider the shortcomings of the 2016 polls. Moreover, Biden's lead at this point is larger than Clinton's in 2016. How should we aggregate all this information to form an opinion about who will win the election? Do those who believe that Biden will win know this, or are those who do not believe it justified in their skeptical attitude?

That is a hard case, a case where it is not easy to say whether we have knowledge or whether skepticism is justified. Then there are also controversial cases. Controversial cases are not the same as hard cases. Some controversial cases are hard, but some are not. Here is a short list of controversial cases: Do we know whether abortion is morally permissible? Do we know whether abortion should be legally permissible? Do we know whether the death penalty is morally permissible? Do we know whether the death penalty should be legally permissible? Do we know whether the Darwinian theory of evolution presents a picture of life on Earth that is more plausible than Biblical creationism? Do we know whether we are witnessing an unprecedented period of human-made global warming? Some of those cases are hard in addition to being controversial, but some are merely controversial. To put (some of) our cards on the table, we think that we do know that the Darwinian theory of evolution is more plausible than Biblical creationism and that we are witnessing a period of unprecedented human-made global warming, and that it is unjustified to maintain a skeptical attitude with respect to those questions, for instance.

So, to go back to our second question, we think it matters a great deal whether skeptics are right. For if skeptics are right, then not only do we not know in any of the controversial cases that we just mentioned, or in the hard cases, but we also do not know even in those cases that everybody would automatically classify as easy. If the more radical skeptics are right, for instance, then we do not even know that it is raining outside when we ourselves are seeing the rain—let alone when our friend tells us so.

So, to go back to our first question: Are the skeptics right? That is what the second part of this book is about. There, we discuss three kinds of philosophical skepticism. According to the first kind, skepticism about induction, although we may know all sorts of things to which we have direct access (for instance, we can know that it is raining when we see the rain), we do not know any of the things that we believe on the basis of inferences which *might* go wrong. According to this sort of skepticism, for instance, we not only do not know whether Biden will win the election but we also do not know whether bread will continue to nourish us or whether the sun will come out tomorrow. The second kind of skepticism, Cartesian skepticism, goes beyond inductive skepticism and holds that although we may know the contents of our own minds (for instance, you may know that it seems to you that you are reading a book right now), we do not know anything about "the external world": you do not know that you have a book in your hands, or indeed even that you have hands. As radical as Cartesian skepticism is, it does not hold a candle to the third kind of skepticism we discuss: Pyrrhonian skepticism. The Pyrrhonian skeptic holds that we know nothing at all. Not even that Pyrrhonian skepticism is true? That is right: according to the Pyrrhonian skeptics, we do not know that Pyrrhonian skepticism is true—which, as we will see, raises some interesting questions.

What is interesting about these three kinds of skepticism is that there are apparently good arguments for them. Anybody can claim that we do not know that we have hands even when we are looking right at them, but we would be well within our rights to dismiss them if they are *just* claiming that. Skeptics, however, hold that skepticism follows from some assumptions which we ourselves hold. If that is true, then we are in a difficult position, because we hold that philosophical skepticism is not justified but we also hold some assumptions from where it follows that philosophical skepticism is justified. We examine the main arguments for the three kinds of philosophical skepticism and the main responses to them that have been offered throughout the history of thought on this topic. We ourselves believe, together with most contemporary philosophers, that the three kinds of philosophical skepticism that we consider are not justified. But although we do not shy away from stating our position when we have it (we think, for instance, that despite his popularity among many scientists, Popper was completely wrong in his "solution" to the problem of induction), the truth is that in many of these cases we think that the skeptics are wrong, but we are not sure exactly where they go wrong. What we aim to do is to give you the tools that you will need to grapple for yourself with these issues.

The skeptics hold that we do not have nearly as much knowledge as think we do. But what is knowledge? That is the question to which the first part of this book is dedicated. As you will see, this is not an easy question to answer, and it quickly gives rise to a number of subsidiary questions, such as "What is truth?", "What is belief?", "What is justification?", and even "Why think that we could even answer the question about knowledge to begin with?" You will also see that, in the end, we do not find a complete and satisfactory answer to the question that we began with—what is knowledge? As before, what we intend to do in this part is to give you the tools that you will need to think for yourself about these issues. In this part, we also introduce many distinctions and arguments that will be very useful for the second part.

You might think that having failed to give a complete and satisfactory answer to the question "What is knowledge?" in the first part, it does not make sense to go on to ask in the second part how much of it we have. This sort of objection was levelled against Socrates himself. In Plato's *Meno*, Socrates is interrogating the titular character regarding the nature of virtue. Meno tries different definitions of that concept, and Socrates presents counterexample after counterexample against each of them. At some point, Meno confronts Socrates with the question: if, as you claim, you do not know what virtue is, how can you be so sure that it is not one of the things I said it is? Similarly, if we do not know what knowledge is, how can we go on to examine how much of it we have? Socrates' own answer in the *Meno* involves the Platonic theory of recollection (itself a theory of knowledge, although not one we deal with here). But there is a more mundane answer that Socrates could have given. To know that kicking puppies just for fun is not a virtuous action, one need not know a complete definition of virtuous action. Therefore, if a proposed definition of virtuous action has the consequence that kicking puppies just for fun is virtuous, then one can know that the definition is defective without oneself knowing the correct definition. Similarly, we can debate how much knowledge we have without ourselves having a complete definition of knowledge, for we can know that a view has unacceptable consequences without knowing what the right view is.

In sum, in this book, we cover some of the main views and arguments regarding two topics: what is knowledge and how much of it we have. There are, of course, many more epistemologically inter-esting topics, and even many more philosophically interesting things to say about those two topics, but we hope that what we cover in this little book will give you a good idea of what epistemology is, and why many people (ourselves most certainly included) find it fascinating.

PART I
Knowledge

INTRODUCTION TO PART I

According to common sense, we know many things and we do not know many others. Some philosophers have held that common sense is wrong in this regard. According to those philosophers, the skeptics, we do not have as much knowledge as we commonly attribute to ourselves. We examine skepticism in the second part of this book. In the first part, we tackle the question of what knowledge is. Remember, however, that, as we said in the Introduction, our search for a definition of knowledge will end up unfinished. Therefore, we do not tackle the question about knowledge before the question about skepticism because we think that you need to know what knowledge is before you know how much of it you have, but because our search for a definition of knowledge, despite delivering incomplete results, will furnish us with many conceptual tools that will be very useful for our discussion of skepticism.

We start by explaining a traditional distinction between three kinds of knowledge: direct knowledge (of things, persons, and places, for instance), know-how (such as knowing how to ride a bike), and propositional knowledge (such as knowing that lions are mammals). We then turn to an attempt to define propositional knowledge in terms of the notions of truth, belief, and justification. In explaining this traditional definition, we also clarify some of the main theories about those concepts. Finally, we consider one of the most influential episodes in contemporary epistemology: Gettier's critique of the proposed definition of propositional knowledge. We consider Gettier's original objections, some of the early proposals for how to deal with it together with reasons for thinking that those proposals do not work, and finally we end with a consideration of what has been called "the Gettier problem problem." The Gettier problem is the problem of trying to come up with a correct definition of propositional knowledge in the face of Gettier's objections to the traditional definition. As our survey of attempted solutions suggests, there is no consensus on how to solve the Gettier problem. The Gettier problem problem, then, consists in asking why this is so: why we have not been able to solve the Gettier problem. In considering the Gettier problem problem, we introduce three traditional distinctions: the analytic/synthetic distinction, the *a priori/a posteriori* distinction, and the necessary/contingent distinction. We do this because a famous critique of these distinctions due to Willard Van Orman Quine opens the doors for one kind of answer to the Gettier problem problem: we cannot find a correct definition of propositional knowledge because the project of trying to come up with definitions of that kind is misguided to begin with. Not everyone accepts Quine's objections, however, and so we end the chapter with a different kind of solution to the Gettier problem problem, one provided by the program of "knowledge-first epistemology." According to this program, pioneered by Timothy Williamson, we cannot find a correct definition of propositional knowledge because knowledge is more basic than the things in whose terms we are trying to define it. Thus, rather than trying to explain knowledge in more basic terms, according to this view we should instead use the notion of knowledge to explain other phenomena. We end this first part of the book with a critical examination of this very influential piece of twenty-first-century epistemology.

1

KINDS OF KNOWLEDGE

INTRODUCTION: THREE KINDS OF KNOWLEDGE

Before encountering skeptical arguments, we would all say that we ourselves, as well as others, know a lot of things. For instance, some of us know Chicago, know how to type, and know that the radius of the Earth is approximately 4,000 miles. Those three cases exemplify three different kinds of knowledge. When we say that we know Chicago, we mean that we have been in that city (or, perhaps more precisely, in enough parts of that city for an appropriate amount of time—having been only at the airport, for instance, may not count as knowing the city); similarly, when we say that we know a person, we mean that we have seen him or her, or that he or she has been introduced to us. In both cases, we are dealing with something which we can call *direct knowledge*:

> **Direct knowledge**: we have direct knowledge of a person, place, or thing just in case we have been in contact with that person, place, or thing.

Some languages mark direct knowledge lexicographically. In Spanish, for instance, we say "conocemos Chicago"—"sabemos Chicago" is not grammatically correct—but English does not have this advantage.

When we say that we know how to type or how to ride a bike, what we mean is that we are capable of doing something, that we have certain *abilities*—it is sometimes called a "know-how":

DOI: 10.4324/9781003208440-3

Knowledge by ability: we know how to do X when we have the ability to do X.

We should be careful when we talk about abilities, because there are ambiguities involved in that talk. Lots of people have the ability to ride a bike in the sense that they have the capacity to learn how to ride a bike, but we would not say of someone who has the ability in this sense that they already know how to ride a bike.

It is clear that direct knowledge and knowledge by ability are different phenomena. There could, of course, be interesting causal connections between know-how and direct knowledge. For instance, to know Chicago, it is usually necessary to have a bunch of abilities, like the ability to drive (if that is how you will get to Chicago), and it would be very difficult to know how to ride a bike without having direct knowledge of any bike. But when we say that direct knowledge and know-how are different, we do not mean to deny these causal relations: what we mean is that having direct knowledge does not consist in having any ability, and that having an ability does not consist in having any direct knowledge. An analogy might help here. There are important correlations between studying hard and passing an exam: students who pass exams usually study hard for them, and students who study hard usually pass exams, but we do not confuse the studying with the passing. Similarly, although direct knowledge and know-how may very well be strongly correlated with each other, we should not confuse them.

Lastly, when we say that we know that the Earth is approximately 4,000 miles we are attributing to ourselves a know-that, or *propositional knowledge*—so-called because in assertions of the kind "We know that . . ." what follows the "that" clause expresses a proposition (we say more about propositions later—for now, it will be sufficient to think of a proposition simply as the complement of a "that" clause). We do not now propose a definition of propositional knowledge because the search for that definition is the main topic of this part of the book. Just as we said that direct knowledge is different from know-how, the traditional position is that propositional knowledge is yet a third kind of knowledge, and that no one of the three kinds of knowledge can be reduced to any of the others—in particular, knowledge by ability is not reducible to propositional knowledge. This position was defended by Gilbert Ryle in *The Concept of Mind*, where he called it "Anti-Intellectualism." According to Ryle, to know how to do something does not consist simply in knowing facts about how to do it. According to the Intellectualist, on the other hand, to know how to ride a bike is to know certain facts about bike-riding (for instance, to initiate a left-hand turn, you have to turn the handlebars slightly to the right), whereas according to Ryle and other Anti-Intellectualists knowing how to ride a bike is completely unrelated to knowing those sorts of facts. More generally:

Intellectualism: To know how to do X is to have propositional knowledge about how to do X.
Anti-Intellectualism: To know how to do X is not to have propositional knowledge about how to do X.

INTELLECTUALISM VERSUS ANTI-INTELLECTUALISM ABOUT KNOW-HOW

ARGUMENTS FOR ANTI-INTELLECTUALISM

Ryle had several arguments for his Anti-Intellectualist position. The Intellectualist asserts that to know how to X just is to have some propositional knowledge about how to X. An identification of a kind of thing A with a different kind of thing B can go wrong in two ways: there can be As that are not Bs, and there can be Bs that are not As. For instance, the identification of dogs with Basenjis is wrong because, even though all Basenjis are dogs, some dogs are not Basenjis (logicians and philosophers say that being a dog is not a sufficient condition for being a Basenji, although it is a necessary condition), whereas the identification of dogs with mammals is wrong because, although all dogs are mammals, not all mammals are dogs (again, logicians and philosophers would say that being a dog is not a necessary condition for being a mammal, although it is a sufficient condition). Of course, a proposed identification can be wrong for both reasons at the same time, as is the identification of dogs with hairless animals (not all dogs are hairless and not all hairless animals are dogs—being a dog is neither necessary nor sufficient for being a hairless animal). (Moreover, identifying the As with the

Bs can be wrong even if all As are Bs and all Bs are As. For instance, even though every creature with a heart is a creature with a kidney and vice versa, it would be wrong to identify the property of having a heart with the property of having a kidney.) Ryle himself did not directly argue that propositional knowledge is not sufficient for know-how (although it would seem easy to come up with examples of that sort, and we will do that momentarily), but he did argue that having propositional knowledge is not necessary for know-how. He also gave a more complicated argument, known as "Ryle's regress." In this section, we consider those three arguments. Later, we will examine what an Intellectualist could say in reply.

Let us start, then, with the claim that having propositional knowledge of the right sort is not a sufficient condition for having the corresponding know-how. That claim could be backed up with some simple examples. Someone who does not know how to ride a bike may well have all sorts of propositional knowledge related to bike-riding: that you have to maintain your center of gravity more or less over the bike, that you have to press the pedals with your feet, etc. It may even happen that someone who does not know how to ride a bike has *more* propositional knowledge about riding bikes than someone who does know how to ride. For instance, if you ask people who know how to ride bikes to explain how to initiate a right-hand side turn, many will tell you that you turn the handlebars to the right. That, however, is not correct. Counterintuitively, you initiate a right turn by steering left. Somebody may well possess that bit of information without knowing how to ride a bike. For another example, someone who is not a very good tennis player may nevertheless have a great deal of propositional knowledge regarding how to play tennis well.

Moreover, turning now to the second argument against intellectualism, the contrary also seems possible: it is perfectly possible for a four-year-old to know how to ride a bike without having any (or almost any) propositional knowledge about it, and a good tennis player need not have much of any propositional knowledge about it. Ryle himself gave other examples:

> The wit, when challenged to cite the maxims, or canons, by which he constructs and appreciates jokes, is unable to answer. He knows how to

make good jokes and how to detect bad ones, but he cannot tell us or himself any recipes for them. So the practice of humour is not a client of its theory. The canons of aesthetic taste, of tactful manners and of inventive technique similarly remain unpropounded without impediment to the intelligent exercise of those gifts.

(Ryle, *The Concept of Mind*, p. 30)

The third kind of argument against intellectualism, "Ryle's regress," goes as follows. Ryle holds that in order to know a proposition you have to think about it—you have to "consider" it, Ryle says. Thus, to know that the radius of the Earth is approximately 4,000 miles, you first have to have thought about that proposition—you cannot know that a proposition is true if you have never considered it. But, according to Ryle, considering a proposition is itself an ability that can be possessed to different degrees by different individuals. Therefore, given that having a bit of propositional knowledge requires considering a proposition, know-how cannot be identified with propositional knowledge on pain of regress.

Let us give an example to see how Ryle's regress would apply to it. Suppose that Jane knows how to ride a bike:

1.   Jane knows how to ride a bike.

According to the Intellectualist, Jane's ability to ride a bike consists in her knowing a proposition about bike-riding. Let us not concern ourselves with exactly what that proposition is, and let us simply note that, according to intellectualism, 1 entails something like the following:

2.   Jane knows that P is true.

But, Ryle now argues, knowing a proposition involves considering that proposition, and to consider a proposition is itself an ability. Therefore, Ryle thinks that 2 entails:

3.   Janes knows how to consider P.

And now the Intellectualist will once again say that Jane's ability described in 3 consists in her knowing a proposition—this time, not a proposition about bike-riding, but a different proposition Q about considering proposition P:

4.   Jane knows that Q is true.

This launches Ryle's regress. Because now Ryle would say that, just as knowing that P entails considering P, knowing Q entails considering Q:

5.   Jane knows how to consider Q.

And, given that the Intellectualist would insist that Jane's ability to consider Q consists in her knowing yet a third proposition R, Ryle concludes that, according to intellectualism, having even the simple ability to ride a bike involves an infinitude of both propositional knowledge and abilities. But this cannot be right—if riding a bike did involve those twin infinite hierarchies, it would be hard to see how anyone could ever ride a bike. Or, at least, so Ryle argued.

ARGUMENT FOR INTELLECTUALISM

But there are also Intellectualist philosophers, according to whom know-how can indeed be identified with propositional knowledge. One motivation for intellectualism is an analogy between attributions of know-how and attributions of propositional knowledge. Consider, for instance, the following list:

1.   John knows when the class starts.
2.   Mary knows who ate the cookie.
3.   Simon knows where the diamonds are.
4.   Sue knows how to ride a bike.

The traditional analysis of the first three elements of that list appeals to propositional knowledge: that John knows when the meeting starts means that John knows a proposition of the form *The meeting starts at . . .*; that Mary knows who ate the cookie means that Mary knows a proposition of the form *. . . ate the cookie*; that Simon knows where the diamonds are means that Simon knows a proposition of the form *The diamonds are . . .*. Intellectualists argue that, following this analogy, we should understand that to say that Sue knows how to ride a bike is to say that Sue knows a proposition of the form . . . *is a way of riding a bike.*

INTELLECTUALIST REPLIES TO THE ARGUMENTS FOR ANTI-INTELLECTUALISM

Is Propositional Knowledge Sufficient for Having an Ability?

But what do Intellectualist say about the Anti-Intellectualist arguments mentioned earlier? Regarding the claim that one can have however much propositional knowledge one wants without having the required ability (for instance, the ability to ride a bike), Intellectualists reply that propositional knowledge is sometimes mediated by *modes of presentation* of a proposition.

What are modes of presentation of a proposition? The concept is best introduced by example. For instance, suppose that John is shopping at a supermarket and notices a trail of sugar on the floor (the example is from Perry, although we use it for a somewhat different purpose). John knows that the shopper with a torn sack of sugar is making a mess. Unbeknownst to John, he himself is the shopper with the torn sack. Now, according to some philosophers, the proposition that the shopper with a torn sack is making a mess is the same as the proposition that John is making a mess. So, does John know this proposition? Well, some philosophers answer, propositional knowledge is not a binary relation between a subject and a proposition, but rather a ternary relation between a subject, a proposition, and a mode of presentation:

> **Mode of presentation of a proposition**: a mode of presentation of a proposition is a way of thinking about that proposition. A single proposition can have multiple modes of presentation.

So, John knows the proposition in question under the mode of presentation *The shopper with a torn sack is making a mess*, but not under the mode of presentation *I am making a mess*. Intellectualists can adopt the thesis that propositional knowledge includes a mode of presentation to answer one of the Anti-Intellectualist arguments as follows: while it is possible to have all sorts of propositional knowledge about how to do something under some modes of presentation without having the corresponding ability, to have the ability is to have propositional knowledge under a *practical* mode of presentation. One can know intellectually all sorts of facts about riding a bike without knowing how to ride a bike, but if one knows those same facts under a practical mode of presentation, then one knows how to ride a bike. Intellectualists do not say much about what a practical mode of presentation is, so this reply to Ryle is to that extent programmatic. Some have argued that if Jane knows how to ride a bike, then she must know a proposition of the following sort: "*this* is how you ride a bike" (where "this" refers to an episode of bike-riding performed by Jane herself).

Intellectualist Reply to Ryle's Regress

What about Ryle's regress argument against intellectualism? Some have argued that Ryle's argument fails because propositional knowledge can be manifested without considering the proposition in question. Ginet, for instance, says:

> I exercise (or manifest) my knowledge that one can get the door open by turning the knob and pushing it (as well as my knowledge that there is a door there) by performing that operation quite automatically as I leave the room; and I may do this, of course, without formulating (in my mind or out loud) that proposition or any other relevant proposition.
>
> (Ginet (1975), p. 7)

According to Ginet, then, Ryle was simply wrong in assuming that having propositional knowledge that such-and-such is the case requires considering the proposition that such-and-such is the case. For instance, Ginet claims, we can know that we can open the door by turning the knob without ever considering the proposition that we can open the door by turning the knob. The very fact that we do in fact open the door by turning the knob demonstrates, according to Ginet, two things: one, that we know how to open the door, and two, that we know that the door can be opened by turning the knob. Thus, Ginet would stop Ryle's regress right at the start: Jane can know that *this* is how you ride a bike without having to consciously consider that proposition.

Is Having Propositional Knowledge Necessary for Having an Ability?

The Anti-Intellectualist argues that one can have propositional knowledge about how to do something without having the corresponding ability to do that thing, and some Intellectualists reply to that argument by appealing to practical modes of presentation of propositions. But Ryle had also argued that one can have the ability without having any propositional knowledge—it seems that one can, for instance, know how to ride a bike without knowing any fact about how to ride bikes. To answer this argument, the Intellectualist can once again appeal to Ginet's distinction between considering a proposition and manifesting one's knowledge of the proposition. The four-year-old does not consider any proposition about how to ride a bike, and certainly cannot verbalise any propositional knowledge of that sort, but if one follows Ginet one can say that even the four-year-old manifests his knowledge that *this* is a way to ride a bike by performing the action referred to by "this."

SUMMARY

In this chapter, we introduced the idea that knowledge comes in different kinds. We can have direct knowledge when we know a person, place, or thing by having direct contact with that person, place, or thing. We can also have abilities, as when we know how to ride a bike or how to type. Finally, we can have propositional knowledge when we know that a certain proposition is true. But is having an ability really different from having propositional knowledge? This is the question on which Intellectualists and Anti-Intellectualists disagree—the former think that know-how just is propositional knowledge, whereas the latter think that they are different things. Anti-Intellectualists like Ryle think that propositional knowledge is neither necessary nor sufficient for know-how, and that Intellectualism leads to a problematic regress. Intellectualists, for their part, think that they can answer these arguments by appealing to the idea of a mode of presentation of a proposition, as well as by denying that knowing that a proposition is true involves a separate intellectual act of considering that proposition. Our focus in the chapters that follow will be on propositional knowledge.

The dispute between Intellectualists and Anti-Intellectualists is thus relevant to what follows because if Intellectualists are right, then everything we say about propositional knowledge in what follows should hold for know-how as well, whereas if Anti-Intellectualists are right it need not. The following exercise is therefore an interesting one for you to undertake: is everything we say in what follows true of know-how as well as of propositional knowledge?

FURTHER READING

An early argument for Intellectualism can be found in Zeno Vendler, *Res Cogitans* (1972), Cornell University Press.

For a book-length discussion of knowledge-how, see J. Adam Carter and Ted Poston, *A Critical Introduction to Knowledge-How* (2018), Bloomsbury.

For a more recent defense of Intellectualism, see Jason Stanley and Timothy Williamson, "Knowing How", *The Journal of Philosophy* 98(8) (2001).

For a thorough introduction to Intellectualism vs. Anti-Intellectualism about know-how, see Jeremy Fantl, "Know-How", in Edward N. Zalta (ed.), *Stanford Encyclopedia of Philosophy* (Fall 2017 edition), https://plato.stanford.edu/archives/fall2017/entries/knowledge-how/.

Ginet's defense of Intellectualism appears in his *Knowledge, Perception, and Memory* (1975), Reidel Publishing Company.

Ryle's defense of Anti-Intellectualism about know-how appears in the second chapter of his *The Concept of Mind* (1949), Hutchinson. This book is not written at an introductory level.

The case of the messy shopper appears in John Perry, "The Problem of the Essential Indexical", *Noûs* 13(1) (1979), pp. 3–21.

THE TRIPARTITE CONCEPTION OF KNOWLEDGE

INTRODUCTION

In the previous chapter, we distinguished between direct knowledge, know-how, and propositional knowledge—and we also explained the controversy between Intellectualists and Anti-Intellectualists regarding whether know-how is simply a species of propositional knowledge. In this chapter, we set aside direct knowledge and know-how to tackle the question: what is propositional knowledge? The name of this chapter, The Tripartite Conception of Knowledge, refers to a traditional answer to that question, one according to which for a subject to know a proposition three conditions must be satisfied: the proposition must be true, the subject must believe the proposition, and the subject's belief in the proposition must be justified.

THE TRIPARTITE CONCEPTION OF KNOWLEDGE

S knows that p if and only if:

1. p is true;
2. S believes that p;
3. S is justified in believing that p.

According to the tripartite conception of knowledge, each of the three conditions is individually necessary for propositional knowledge, and the three of them taken together are collectively sufficient. What it means to say that each condition is individually necessary

DOI: 10.4324/9781003208440-4

is that for a subject to know a proposition, the proposition must be true, the subject must believe it, and the subject must be justified in believing it. If *any* of those conditions fails to be satisfied, then the subject does not know the proposition. What it means to say the three conditions are collectively sufficient is that if a subject has a justified belief in a true proposition, then the subject knows that proposition.

Compare the tripartite conception of knowledge with the following definition of a vixen:

Something x is a vixen if and only if:

1. x is a fox;
2. x is female.

According to that definition, being a fox and being a female are individually necessary for being a vixen: nothing can be a vixen without being a female, and nothing can be a vixen without being a fox. Also, according to that definition, being both a fox and a female are together sufficient for being a vixen: anything that is both a fox and a female is a vixen. The idea of the tripartite conception is that just as being a female fox is necessary and sufficient for being vixen, so too being a true justified belief is necessary and sufficient for being a piece of propositional knowledge.

In this chapter, we analyze the individual components of this definition: truth, belief, and justification. As we will see, each of these concepts gives rise to interesting philosophical issues.

THE TRUTH CONDITION

A fundamental difference between beliefs (about which we will talk in the next section) and knowledge is that whereas beliefs can be false, there is no such thing as false knowledge. Some people believed (and some still do!) that the Earth is flat. Why do they not know it? The answer to this question may well be overdetermined, but one clear reason why they do not know it is that it is not true that the Earth is flat: that is to say, because the truth condition is not satisfied. Some people will sometimes attribute knowledge of false propositions when the subject is firmly convinced of the truth of the proposition in question, but this seems to be a metaphorical (not literal) use of "knowledge," more or less synonymous with "firmly believes." Thus, for instance, when someone says that they "knew" that they were going to win the lottery (despite the fact that they did not), we can see that they are using "know" in a derivative way.

TRUTH-BEARERS

But what is truth? According to the Bible, this question was famously posed by Pontius Pilate to Jesus Christ (apparently Pilate left the room before Jesus had a chance to reply). Before figuring out what truth is, we need to figure out what kinds of things can be true—what kinds of things are "truth-bearers," as the terminology goes.

> **Truth-bearer**: a truth-bearer is something that can be true or false.

The tripartite conception of knowledge itself presupposes that beliefs are truth-bearers, but they are not the only candidates. Other truth-bearers that have been proposed in the literature include sentences (of natural as well as of artificial languages), statements, propositions, assertions, etc. With the aim of imposing a minimum of discipline to our discussion, we will deal only with three truth-bearers: sentences, propositions, and beliefs.

Let us start with sentences. What is a sentence?

> **Sentence**: a sentence is a chain of expressions of a language, grammatically correct and complete.

For instance, "Snow is white," "Close the window," and "What time is it?" are sentences of English. Philosophers usually distinguish between sentence-types and sentence-tokens. A sentence-token is a physical object, a succession of marks on papers or of sound waves. When two or more tokens are considered as emissions (that is to say, as inscriptions or utterances) of the same sentence, "the same sentence" means *the same sentence-type*. For instance, the following two inscriptions:

All men are mortal.
All men are mortal.

are two tokens of the same type. A sentence-type is sometimes understood as a model exemplified by its tokens, and sometimes simply as a class of similar tokens.

We can also make the traditional grammatical distinctions within the class of sentences. For instance, we can distinguish between declarative, interrogative, imperative, and exclamatory sentences. This distinction allows us to see that not all kinds of sentences are good candidates for truth-bearers. In general, non-declarative sentences are neither true nor false. Questions can be polite or rude, intelligent or banal, etc., but not true or false. And yet, are we not all aware of rhetorical questions? Running the risk of ruining an already pretty bad joke, rhetorical questions show us that, simply because a sentence has the superficial syntactical structure of a question, that does not mean that it cannot be used to convey information—that it cannot be a truth-bearer. On the other hand, it is not obvious that all declarative sentences are truth-bearers. Some metaphors, for instance, are expressed by declarative sentences, and it is not obvious that all of them are either true or false (which does not mean that they cannot be more or less adequate, nor does it mean that we are denying the existence of dead metaphors which can be true or false). Another interesting case is that of sentences with false existential presuppositions. The soccer World Cup is played every four years, and it was not played in 1980. Armed with that information, what do you think about the following sentence: "The winner of the 1980 soccer World Cup was a European team"? It is certainly not true, but do you think it is false? Or do you think that it is neither true nor false? Whatever you think, you are in good company, because there are philosophers who would say that it is false, and there are other philosophers who would say that it is neither true nor false. If these latter philosophers are right, then we have here another counterexample to the thesis that all declarative sentences are truth-bearers. Two other potential counterexamples are vague sentences ("She is tall," said of someone not clearly tall but not clearly not tall either), and sentences about so-called "future contingents" ("It will rain tomorrow").

It looks, then, like the grammatical criterion for figuring out whether a sentence is a truth-bearer will not work. That is to say, just because a sentence is declarative, we cannot assume that it is a truth-bearer, and just because it is not declarative, we cannot assume that it is not a truth-bearer. If not its grammatical properties, what then determines whether a sentence is a truth-bearer? We can now introduce our second truth-bearer candidate: propositions. Before we said that we could think of a proposition simply as the complement of the "that" clause in an attribution of knowledge. Now we can give a more substantial definition:

Proposition: the meaning (or content) of those sentences which can be true or false.

Given this understanding of "proposition," it will be simply true by definition that a sentence is a truth-bearer if and only if it expresses a proposition. Therefore, it seems like we have not advanced much: we can now say that the sentences which are truth-bearers are exactly those which express propositions, but we have no independent grip on the notion of what a proposition is besides the fact that they are the meaning of truth-bearing sentences.

But we have made *some* progress, for we can now ask: what kind of meaning must a sentence have for it to make sense to say that it is a truth-bearer? And we can then introduce a theory of what propositions are to answer that question. The theory that we will talk about is by no means universally accepted, but it is at least a "minimal" conception, in the sense that pretty much everyone will accept that propositions are *at least* what this theory says they are—although many will want to add that they are *more* than what this theory says they are.

According to this theory, a proposition is a representation or a "picture" of reality. More specifically, we can say that a proposition allows us to *distinguish possibilities*. If something is possible, then there is a proposition that is true exactly of those occasions where the possibility obtains, and false otherwise. For instance, it is possible that Jack the Ripper was a doctor. Therefore, there is a proposition that is true if and only if Jack the Ripper was a doctor. Some possibilities are actual: Chicago is in Illinois, and so it is possible that Chicago is in Illinois (although it may sound weird if you *say* just that it is possible when you know that it is true). Therefore, there is a proposition which is true if and only if Chicago is in Illinois—and that proposition is true. Some possibilities, on the other hand, are not actual: Jorge Luis Borges was not a lawyer, but he could have been (few Argentinians are not). Therefore, there is a proposition that is true if and only if Borges was a lawyer—and that proposition is false.

Notice that the view that propositions distinguish possibilities allows us to explain why non-rhetorical questions and orders are not truth-bearers: non-rhetorical questions do not allow you to distinguish possibilities (although answers to them may), and neither do orders (rather, they do something like instructing the hearer to actualise a possibility). In addition, that view of propositions also allows us to distinguish between sentences that are truth-bearers and the propositions they express. For two different sentences may distinguish the same possibilities. Thus, consider the sentences "Ronaldo kicked the ball" and "The ball was kicked by Ronaldo." They are different sentences—for instance, they begin with different words—but they distinguish the same possibilities: those were Ronaldo kicked the ball from those where he did not. When that happens, we say that the sentences express the same proposition— and, therefore, they will be either both true or both false. Another source of examples of different sentences expressing the same proposition is given by translations: for instance, the sentences "It is raining," "Es regnet," and "Está lloviendo" all express the same proposition (in English, German, and Spanish, respectively). They do so because each of them distinguishes the same possibilities: those where it is raining from those where it is not.

So, two sentences can express the same proposition. Is the reverse also possible—can a single sentence express different propositions? The answer to this question is a bit more complicated, and we will not get into the details of the philosophy of language that would be required to give a complete answer. But, at least in principle, it would seem possible for a single sentence-type to express two propositions, and so-called "indexical" expressions provide one source of potential examples. Thus, for instance, the sentence "I am hungry" as uttered by Sue expresses the proposition that Sue is hungry, whereas the same sentence uttered by Joe expresses the proposition that Joe is hungry. Besides pronouns such as "I," "He," "She," "They," etc., other indexical expressions include "here" and "there" (although arguably not "everywhere"), as well as "Yesterday," "Today," and "Tomorrow," "This," "That," etc.

We have a relatively clear understanding of what a sentence is, but we sharply distinguished between sentences and propositions.

Even those sentences that are truth-bearers are not *identical* to propositions, but rather "express" propositions. A proposition, after all, is the meaning of some sentences, and we need to distinguish between the meaning and the vehicle used to express that meaning. What then are propositions? On a minimal interpretation, they are simply ways of distinguishing possibilities, nothing more and nothing less. There is still, of course, the question of what these ways exactly are, but for our purposes here we do not need to get into that metaphysical issue.

Just as sentences can be truth-bearers derivatively, by expressing propositions, the same happens with our third candidate truth-bearers: beliefs. If we go back to the tripartite conception of knowledge, we can see that it itself mentions propositions. The variable "p" in that characterisation is naturally interpreted as a propositional variable. To have propositional knowledge, it is not necessary to speak any language in particular—and maybe it is not necessary to speak any language at all. A belief, then, can be true in the same derivative sense in which a sentence can be true: in virtue of having as its content a true proposition. The relationship between a belief and a proposition is in many ways (though of course not in all ways) like the relationship between a sentence and a proposition. Just as different sentences can express the same proposition, different beliefs can have the same proposition as its content (two people, for instance, can (and often do) believe the same thing). Thus, the proposition that Mount Kilimanjaro is over 19,000 feet tall can be expressed by different sentences (for instance, in different languages) as well as believed by different people.

We now have a clearer understanding of what kinds of things can be true or false—but we still need to figure out what we mean when we say, for example, that it is true that Chicago is in Illinois.

CLASSICAL THEORIES OF TRUTH

What must happen for a truth-bearer to be true? Any answer to that question constitutes what in philosophical terminology is called a "theory of truth." In this section, we will examine three "classical" theories of truth—Correspondentism, Coherentism, and Pragmatism.

Here is, first, a brief characterisation of the three classical theories. For *correspondence* theories, truth is a matter of a relation between a truth-bearer and reality—a truth-bearer is true if and only if it "corresponds" to a fact. For *coherence* theories, a belief is true only insofar as it is part of a system of beliefs, and its truth consists in a certain relation of coherence with the other beliefs in the system. For *pragmatic* theories, truth is "what works" or what will be accepted at the end of inquiry (depending on the brand of Pragmatism in question).

TRUTH AS CORRESPONDENCE

The idea of truth as correspondence to reality is perhaps the oldest one, and it can be found in a more or less explicit form in Aristotle and St. Thomas Aquinas. The correspondence theory, narrowly conceived, is committed to an ontology of facts. Thus, for the correspondence theory, it is true that Miles plays the trumpet because there is a fact (a fact which has as components at least Miles and trumpets) to which that proposition corresponds, whereas it is not true that John plays the trumpet because there is no corresponding fact.

One objection to correspondence theories is based on this narrow construal of it, and it has to do with dissatisfaction with an ontology of facts. In particular, some authors have felt uncomfortable with the alleged consequence of the correspondence theory that there are strange kinds of facts, such as negative, disjunctive, and universal facts. Take, for instance, the true proposition that London is not in France. Is this proposition true because it corresponds to a negative fact? If so, what fact is that? Some will be tempted to reply: the fact that London is not in France. But this reply gives rise to another related objection to the correspondence theory: that facts are simply the shadow of truth-bearers, and that they do not have independent reality. What is meant by this is that when pressed to say which fact corresponds to a certain true proposition P, proponents of the correspondence theory cannot do better than simply utter a sentence which expresses the proposition P.

Atomic Versus Molecular Propositions, Recursive Definitions, and Negative Facts

Let us first take up the objection about negative facts—we leave the other objection for our discussion of Deflationism about truth.

The objection, again, is the following: there seems to be no such thing as a negative fact which corresponds to the proposition that London is not in France, and so the correspondence theory would have the wrong consequence that it is not true that London is not in France. The correspondence theorist could reply that we must distinguish between simple (or "atomic," as they are sometimes called) propositions, on the one hand, and complex ("molecular") propositions, on the other. Atoms do not have other atoms as components, whereas molecules are composed of atoms. The idea, then, is that something similar happens with propositions: some are composed of other propositions, whereas some are atomic in that they are not composed of other propositions.

What is the "glue" which binds propositions together into larger molecular propositions? There are certain concepts that play this role, and they are called "connectives"—because they connect propositions to each other to form more complex propositions. Here is a (non-exhaustive) list of propositional connectives:

Some propositional connectives: not, and, or.

These connectives are known, respectively, as negation, conjunction, and disjunction. Thus, for instance, the connective *and* forms the molecular proposition *Chicago is in Illinois and Paris is in France* from the atomic propositions *Chicago is in Illinois* and *Paris is in France*. Why do we say that *Chicago is in Illinois* and *Paris is in France* are atomic? They do, after all, have parts. That is true: the proposition that Chicago is in Illinois, for instance, in some sense involves Chicago and Illinois (or, maybe, concepts that refer to those things). But the proposition that Chicago is in Illinois is atomic because, although it has parts, the parts are not themselves propositions. The same goes for the proposition that France is in Paris. Does this mean that connectives can only form molecular propositions out of atomic propositions? Not at all. Molecular propositions can have as parts propositions which are themselves molecular. Of course, a proposition cannot be molecular "all the way down": the elementary components of a molecular proposition will indeed be atomic propositions, but the intermediate ones need not be.

The idea, then, is that you can start with atomic propositions and form some molecular propositions from them by joining them with some connective, and then you can use these newly formed molecular propositions to form yet larger molecular propositions with them as components, and so on and so forth. Thus, for example, the molecular proposition *Chicago is in Illinois and Paris is not in France* contains as components the atomic proposition *Chicago is in Illinois* and the molecular proposition *Paris is not France*. Notice, by the way, that negation is different from disjunction and conjunction in that it only needs a single proposition as input to deliver a new molecular proposition as output (whereas conjunction and disjunction need two input propositions). This is what is meant by saying that conjunction is a *unary* connective (whereas disjunction and conjunction are *binary* connectives).

To turn this distinction between atomic and molecular propositions into an answer to the objection to the correspondence theory regarding negative facts, we must first talk about recursive definitions. A recursive definition is characterised by the use of three kinds of clauses: base clauses, in which the notion to be defined does not appear, recursive clauses, in which that notion does appear, and, finally, closure clauses. The base and recursive clauses establish sufficient conditions for the application of the notion defined, whereas closure clauses guarantee that, taken all together, the previous clauses offer necessary conditions as well. Thus, for instance, in some countries, citizenship is determined by birth as well as by having a parent who is a citizen. A recursive definition of citizenship for those countries can be given:

Recursive definition of citizenship
Base clause: If S was born in P, then S is a citizen of P.
Recursive clause: If one of S's parents is a citizen of P, then S is a citizen of P.
Closure clause: Only those who satisfy at least one of the previous two clauses is a citizen of P.

Note that the recursive clause requires that S's parents be citizens, not that they be born in the country in question. A clause which required that would grant citizenship only to those who were born in the country and their immediate descendants. On the contrary, the recursive clause grants citizenship to anyone with at least one ancestor born in the country (by the way, the very notion of ancestor can be given a recursive definition). That is why the clause is *recursive*: *S*'s parents can be citizens in virtue of satisfying the base clause (that is to say, in virtue of having been born in the country in question) or in virtue of themselves satisfying the recursive clause (that is to say, in virtue of the citizenship of *their* parents). If this is what happens (that is to say, if *S*'s parents were not born in the country in question, but *their* parents are citizens), then the same goes for *S*'s grandparents: they may be citizens in virtue of having been born in the country or in virtue of having parents who are citizens, and so on and so forth. Of course, this citizenship chain must eventually bottom out in someone who is a citizen in virtue of satisfying the base clause. And this is another characteristic of recursive definitions: the chains may be long, but they always end (or begin) in the base clause.

We can, if we want, give a recursive definition of the notion of proposition:

Recursive definition of proposition (partial)
Base Clause: Any atomic proposition is a proposition.
Recursive Clause: If *A* and *B* are propositions, then so are *not-A*, *Either A or B*, and *A and B*.
Closure Clause: Nothing else is a proposition.

Notice two important things about that recursive definition of proposition: first, it presupposes that you already understand the notion of an atomic proposition, and so it is not intended as giving you a complete understanding of what a proposition is. Rather, it allows us to formalise what we just said about the relationship between atomic and molecular propositions. Second, its recursive clause will surely need to be augmented. There are more connectives than simply negation, disjunction, and conjunction. We use these three in part to simplify matters (and in part because they are, in logicians' terms, a "complete" set of connectives—that is to say, every other "truth-functional" connective can be defined in their terms). That is why we say that the preceding is a partial recursive definition of proposition.

Now we can answer the objection about negative (and conjunctive and disjunctive) facts. The correspondence theorist could say that whereas the truth of atomic propositions is due to their correspondence with a fact, there is no fact that needs to directly correspond to molecular propositions. Rather, the following recursive definition of truth can be offered:

Recursive definition of correspondentist truth (partial)

Base Clause: An atomic proposition is true if and only if it corresponds to the facts.

Recursive Clause: If A and B are propositions, then:

    a.   *Not-A* is true if and only if *A* is not true;

    b.   *A and B* is true if and only if *A* is true and *B* is true;

    c.   *A or B* is true if and only if either *A* is true or *B* is true.

Closure Clause: No other proposition is true.

Again, we need to remember that the recursive clause in this definition will need to be augmented with the other connectives one wishes to countenance (that is why we call it a partial definition). And we also need to remember that the apparent circularity in the appeal to the notion of truth in the recursive clause is not problematic, for the truth of any given proposition will depend, in the end, on whether some atomic propositions correspond to the facts or not.

If Truth Is Correspondence to the Facts, Is Truth Unknowable?

Another sort of objection to the correspondence theory is epistemological in nature. This objection contends that given its stark distinction between truth-bearers and the independent reality they depict, the correspondence theory makes truth unknowable. If truth is correspondence with an independent reality, then to know that a proposition is true we would have to have access to that independent reality. But, given that we can only access our own representations of reality, we can never know that a proposition is true.

This argument, though widespread in some circles, seems to us doubly confused. In the first place, it is not true that a correspondence theory is committed to an *independent* reality. The correspondence theory is committed to a distinction between truth-bearers and that in virtue of which they are true, but whether this reality in virtue of which truth-bearers are true is independent, and what it is independent of, is outside the scope of the correspondence theory as a theory of truth. A subjective idealist like Berkeley could very well hold a correspondence theory. For Berkeley (or for a textbook version of Berkeley which suits our purposes here), reality was not independent of subjective mental states (we talk some more about his theory in Chapter 6). That Miles plays the trumpet was, for instance, a fact that obtained in virtue of what was going on in some mind (perhaps the mind of God). Still, Berkeley could have well held that it is true that Miles plays the trumpet because that proposition corresponds to the (mind-dependent) fact that Miles plays the trumpet.

So, the correspondence theory is not really committed to anything specific about the nature of the reality to which truths correspond. But even if it were, the objection we are considering would still not be a good one. The idea of the objection is that if truth is a matter of correspondence with independently existing reality, then we can never know that a proposition is true because we can never have access to that independent reality. But why not? The objection seems to presuppose that some kind of skepticism (perhaps a Cartesian version) is correct. But whether such skepticism is correct is very much doubtful, as we shall see in the second part of this book, and at any rate cannot simply be presupposed as true in an objection to the correspondence theory.

We have spent a considerable amount of time on the correspondence theory, and you will soon see we will spend relatively little time on the other two classical theories, the coherence theory and the pragmatist theory. This is so for two related reasons. First, the correspondence theory is by far the more developed of the three classical theories. Second, we ourselves are considerably more sympathetic toward the correspondence theory than to its two classical rivals.

Truth as Coherence

The coherence theory denies that truth is a matter of the relationship between truth-bearers and something else—rather, for coherence theories truth is a matter of internal relations among truth-bearers. But what does this relation, "coherence," consist in? In some versions, coherence is simply a matter of consistency. Thus, a belief coheres with a system of belief if and only if it is consistent with it—i.e., if and only if no contradiction can be derived from the system once the belief in question is added to it. Other theories hold that mere consistency is not enough, and that the beliefs in the system in question need to not only be consistent but also bear explanatory relations to each other. Thus, most actual systems of beliefs are not sets of completely unconnected propositions, but rather the beliefs that are part of those systems tend to support each other.

Regardless of how the notion of coherence is to be explained, it would seem clearly possible to construct two alternative belief systems incompatible with each other but each internally coherent. For instance, one system could be built around the belief that Napoleon ate chicken for his twelfth birthday, and another around the belief that he did not. Presumably, only one of those beliefs is true. But then, if we think that those systems really are possible, that shows that coherence theories cannot be right. Perhaps the coherence theorist could reply that the idea that if a proposition is true its negation cannot be false begs the question against the coherence theory. But if accepting the coherence theory implies denying the principle of no contradiction (namely, that it is not possible for a proposition and its negation to both be true), few would be willing to pay that price. Alternatively, the coherence theorist could say that truth is coherence with a system of *actually held* beliefs, and that no one holds those beliefs about Napoleon. But this answer does not seem satisfactory either, for two reasons. First, we could easily change the example so that the beliefs are indeed actually held—plenty of people hold incompatible system of beliefs about what killed the dinosaurs or who wrote the works attributed to Shakespeare, not to mention political and moral disagreements, and it seems like wishful thinking to hope that in *all* of these cases one of the bands has a less coherent system than the others. But second, and more importantly, why is the coherence theory restricted to *actually held* beliefs? If it is possible for a coherent system of beliefs to be built around a proposition, why does it matter whether anyone actually holds those beliefs or not? Why is that not simply an unmotivated maneuver designed only to save the coherence theory?

One argument in favor of the coherence theory is its relation to a coherentist theory of justification (about which we will say more in the second part of this book). According to a coherentist theory of justification, a belief is *justified* if and only if it belongs to a coherent system of beliefs. If, to this theory of justification, we add the thesis that a belief is true if and only if it is justified, then a coherence theory of truth results. But both premises of this argument are subject to serious doubts. As we said, we will talk more about coherentist theories of justification in the second part of this book, but the identification of truth with justified belief is itself hardly acceptable to someone who does not already accept a coherence theory of truth.

Pragmatism About Truth

Pragmatic theories of truth are associated with the American philosophers Charles Peirce and William James. Peirce held that true beliefs are those that will be accepted "at the end of inquiry," whereas James proposed to define truth more broadly in terms of utility. The Peircean idea is that a belief is true if and only if it can withstand all objections to it. A classic objection to the Jamesian account is that true propositions may be useless and useful propositions may be false. A related objection is that pragmatists are offering at best a *criterion* of truth, rather than a definition of it. This objection applies to Peircean as well as to Jamesian conceptions. That a belief will withstand all objections to it, or that it proves itself useful, might be good *indications* that it is true, but even common sense makes a distinction between a good indication of something and the thing itself. Pragmatists themselves may agree with the spirit of these objections, for even James himself seems to have expressed sympathy with the idea that he was not trying to define truth, but rather say something interesting about it. Indeed, James and Peirce did not seem opposed to the correspondence theory of truth as such as much as with its utility. But then, these pragmatist theories are not best described as theories of truth, but rather as theories of the usefulness of truth (or something to that effect).

RELATIVISM REGARDING TRUTH

It is often said that there are no absolute truths, that all truths are relative. Sometimes what someone means by this is correct: what is meant is that beliefs change with time, and that what was believed true yesterday is believed false today, or that what Joe thinks is true Mary thinks is false. All of this is of course correct—it is even something trivial, which everyone knows—but it is expressed in a misleading way by saying that truth is relative. If Joe changes his mind and goes from believing that it will not rain today to believing that it will, that shows that Joe's beliefs are "relative" only in the sense that what Joe believes at one time is not the same as what he believes at another. This need not be something bad on Joe's part, of course: he may be simply responding rationally to additional evidence about the weather. But what Joe believes is not relative. Let us suppose that it will in fact rain today. Then what Joe believed at the outset is false and was always false, whereas what Joe ended up believing is true and was always true. What changed was Joe's attitude toward the proposition that it will rain today, not whether that proposition is true.

But what if what is really meant by saying that all truths are relative is the literal interpretation: not the truism that people sometimes change their mind, but that some propositions themselves can go from being true to being false (or vice versa)? There is one benign way in which this may turn out to be true, but it is not what real relativists have in mind. We explain first the benign sort of relativism, and then the more serious one.

Depending on our exact theory of propositions, it could be admitted that there are some propositions whose truth value can change with changing circumstances. In our discussion of the difference between sentences and propositions, we called attention to the existence of indexical expressions such as "I" and "here." If we admit the existence of indexical propositions as well as indexical sentences, then there can be propositions with changing truth values. Thus, for example, the proposition "It is raining" is true in some circumstances—when it rains in the indicated location—and false in others; the proposition "I have a headache" is true if uttered by Manolo right now and false if uttered by Juan. Anti-relativists are not *forced* to admit this: they can make the identity criterion for propositions so strict that any change in circumstances implies a change in propositions. But this is a relatively esoteric issue in the philosophy of language which we will not address here. Suffice it to say that this restricted form of relativism about truth is not the kind that real relativists find exciting.

Rather, real relativists want to argue that even propositions that do not obviously have any contextual parameters can change their truth value. Thus, for example, take the proposition that it rained on January 21, 1973, in Tucson, Arizona. The truth value of that proposition is not relative for boring reasons—the kinds of reasons for which the truth value of *I am hungry* can be relative, for instance. So could the truth of a proposition like that be relative?

We leave consideration of that question up to you, but we close with two comments on it. First, it is well worth noting that this discussion is only interesting if the notion of truth in question is correspondentist. For coherence and pragmatist theories, relativism regarding truth is true but also trivial: it is obvious, for instance, that one proposition may be useful for one person but not for another, and we already mention the possibility of alternative coherent systems of beliefs, one of which contains one proposition and another its negation. Second, there is one reason for embracing serious relativism about truth that we think is misguided. Some people think that serious relativism about truth is the only tolerant position available. After all, some people believe a proposition and some its negation. If we are anti-relativists, if we think that only one of these people can be right, are we not being intolerant as well—are we not encroaching on the other person's right to believe whatever they want? We think that this is a misguided reason for adopting serious relativism about truth for two reasons. First, it confuses an epistemological question—namely, what is it rational for someone to believe—with the question about truth. It may well be that the two people in question are perfectly rational in believing what they do—for instance, they may have very different evidence, and they may be responding rationally to the evidence they have. But second, and perhaps more importantly, tolerance has little to do with whether all truths are relative. Indeed, real tolerance is reserved for those who we think are wrong. If you believe that abortion is always impermissible and your friend believes that it is sometimes permissible, you tolerate her opinion when you think that she is wrong but do not shun her. If you are a relativist and think that both you and your friend are right, then tolerance is not the right attitude to take toward her opinion. You do not tolerate true opinions, you only tolerate false opinions (or opinions you take to be false). Therefore, if you are inclined to be a relativist about truth because of your respect for tolerance, you should think again.

DEFLATIONISM ABOUT TRUTH

The three classical theories about truth that we examined (the correspondence theory, the coherence theory, and Pragmatism about truth) all agree that truth is a real property of truth-bearers such as propositions—they just disagree about what property that is. But there is an approach to the question about what truth is that disagrees with all these classical theories: that approach has it that there is no substantive property that all true propositions share and in virtue of which they are true. Rather, the truth predicate simply plays some linguistic roles for which there is no need to posit a corresponding property. Because it denies that truth is a substantive property, this view is sometimes known as "Deflationism" about truth: it is "deflating" what it takes to be lofty and unwarranted metaphysical claims made by traditional theories of truth.

Deflationism can be seen as arising from the observation that the truth predicate plays a "disquotational" role. What is meant by this is that there is an equivalence between a sentence S which attributes truth to another sentence S' and the sentence S' itself. Thus, for instance, to say "The sentence 'Snow is white' is true" is equivalent to saying, "Snow is white." Generalising, we have what philosophers and logicians call the T-schema:

T-schema: "S" is true if and only if S.

An instance of the T-schema is obtained by replacing "S" in both of its appearances with the same sentence. Deflationism, to a first approximation, is the view that all there is to say about truth is that every instance of the T-schema is true. Notice that Deflationism says nothing about correspondence, coherence, or utility. Notice too that if the T-schema really were all there is to say about the truth predicate, then the truth predicate is in principle eliminable from the language, for whenever we want to predicate truth of a sentence, we can instead simply assert that very sentence.

That, however, is only a first approximation to Deflationism because there are non-disquotational uses of the truth predicate. For instance, there are "blind" attributions of truth, such as, for example, when Joe does not know what Mary says, but trusts her so much that he says, "Whatever Mary said is true." The truth predicate also seems indispensable for generalising, as when we say, for example, "All the consequences of the Peano axioms are true." More precisely, then, Deflationism is the view that the truth predicate exists simply to play those kinds of roles, and that it does not correspond to any substantive property out there in the world.

What is the relationship between Deflationism and the classical theories of truth we examined earlier? Deflationism is opposed to all of them since they presuppose that truth is a substantive property—correspondence to facts, or coherence, or utility. But there is still a difference between them. The guiding idea in Deflationism seems to be more friendly toward the correspondence theory than to either the coherence or the pragmatist theory of truth. Take, for instance, a simple attribution of truth, like " 'Snow is white' is true." According to Deflationism, that sentence is equivalent to "Snow is white," and that is all there is to say about the function of the truth predicate in it. There is here no room for the coherence of that sentence (or a belief in it) to play any role, nor for the usefulness of it either. But there seems to be some room for the idea that truth results from an asymmetric relation between language and something extralinguistic, and this is certainly one key component of the correspondence theory of truth. If Deflationism is indeed friendly toward the correspondence theory, then it allows that theory to answer concerns about the notion of fact. Remember that one worry about the correspondence theory was that the notion of fact that it employs seemed to be very thin—when asked which fact corresponds to the true (atomic) proposition that P, correspondentists can do no better than to answer that it is the fact that P itself. A correspondentist with deflationary sympathies can take this worry in stride, for she can say that there is indeed nothing more to the notion of facts than their correspondence to true (atomic) propositions in the way indicated by the T-schema.

THE BELIEF CONDITION

Let us now deal with the belief condition. To know something, it is necessary to believe it. This may sound strange, because in many cases believing seems incompatible with knowing. Thus, when we make assertions of the sort "I believe that *p*," we are often recognising that we do not know that *p*; we believe it, but we are not sure. In those cases, "believe" is used in the sense of *tentatively believing*. But that is not how belief is understood in formulating the belief condition. This condition demands that the subject in question believe that *p*, but not that he or she says, "I believe that *p*," and only this latter is sometimes incompatible with knowledge (not always: some people pray, "I firmly believe . . ."). Why did some ancients not know that the Earth is round even though it is? Because they did not believe that it was, they thought it was flat. In this context, belief is also detached from its religious connotations. One can, of course, have beliefs with theological content (for instance, that God exists, or that He does not), but also with any other kind of content. Moreover, it is not at all assumed that belief does not admit of evidence or reasons in its favor—that is to say, belief is not equated with faith. On the contrary, it is assumed that beliefs can indeed be supported by reasons or evidence—and this is indeed the content of the justification condition, which we examine later.

Belief is a special kind of mental state. In the first place, it is a *propositional attitude*, by which we mean that it is a mental state with a content, and that its content is a proposition. Maybe some mental states have no content whatsoever (headaches may be a good candidate, although some philosophers will disagree), and maybe some others have content, but not propositional content (for instance, some philosophers hold that sensory experiences have nonconceptual, hence nonpropositional, content), but many mental states have propositional content. John hopes to play in the concert, Mary wants to eat chocolate, Sue fears that it will rain tomorrow. John, Mary, and Sue, then, are in mental states which can be characterised as propositional attitudes. With more or less effort one can even make that propositional content explicit: John hopes that the proposition *John plays in the concert* be true; Mary wants the proposition *Mary eats chocolate* to be true; Sue fears that the proposition *It's raining* be true tomorrow.

Within the propositional attitudes, we can further distinguish the *doxastic* attitudes. "*Doxa*" means "opinion" in Ancient Greek, so doxastic attitudes are opinion-like propositional attitudes. Belief is a paradigm case of doxastic attitude, but there are others. For instance, disbelief is a doxastic attitude. Or maybe disbelieving that *p* is simply believing that *not-p*, and then disbelief would not be a doxastic attitude different from belief. Be that as it may, there is another doxastic attitude that will be very important in the second part of this book: suspension of judgment. We must be careful to distinguish suspension of judgment as a full-fledged doxastic attitude from the mere absence of taking any attitude toward a proposition. To suspend judgment, in the sense in which we will here use the expression, involves having considered (however implicitly) the proposition and having reached the conclusion that there are not sufficient reasons to consider it true but there are not sufficient reasons to consider it false either. In contrast, if someone has not even considered a proposition, then they do not suspend judgment, but rather take no attitude whatsoever with respect to it. For instance, agnostics suspend judgment with respect to the proposition that God exists, but at least many of them have not even considered the proposition that the number of stars in the Milky Way is even. Think of belief as giving two thumbs up to a proposition, disbelief as giving it two thumbs down, suspension of judgment as one thumb up and one thumb down, and having not considered it as not giving it any thumbs in any direction.

Three doxastic attitudes

Belief: two thumbs up toward a proposition.
Disbelief: two thumbs down toward a proposition.
Suspension of judgment: one thumb up and one thumb down toward a proposition.

Belief, disbelief, and suspension of judgment are examples of coarse-grained doxastic attitudes. In contrast with them, many philosophers think that there are also fine-grained doxastic attitudes. Joe thinks that the Patriots will win the next Superbowl and also that he is eating pasta. But if our description of Joe's mental state is limited to noting that he has those two beliefs, then it is a very poor description. What we are missing is that Joe believes much more

strongly the second proposition than the first one. So far, most philosophers would agree with this. But some philosophers think that
a way to capture this difference is by introducing graded doxastic
attitudes, and that a faithful description of Joe's mental states should
say that he believes *to a high degree* that he is eating pasta, whereas he
adopts a different doxastic attitude, to wit, *believing to a low degree*,
with respect to the proposition that the Patriots will win the next
Superbowl. Some of those philosophers even think that there are an
(innumerably) infinite number of such attitudes, for they hold that
there is one of them for each real number between 0 and 1. The
epistemology of fine-grained attitudes raises some very interesting
questions, but in this book we limit ourselves to the coarse-grained
attitudes of belief, disbelief, and suspension of judgment.

THE JUSTIFICATION CONDITION

What is a belief is a question analyzed in the philosophy of mind,
and what is truth in the philosophy of language or philosophical
semantics. But what is justification is a question that falls squarely
under the purview of epistemology, as the branch of philosophy
which studies questions about knowledge is sometimes called.

Miles thinks that the next flip of his coin will come up heads;
he flips it, and it comes up heads. The belief and the truth conditions are satisfied. Would we say in this case that Miles *knew* that
the coin would come up heads? Normally, no; we would rather say
that he *guessed right*. Why do we not attribute knowledge in cases
like this? Because the justification condition is not satisfied: Miles'
belief that the coin would come up heads, though true, was not a
well-founded or justified belief; it was just based on a feeling. For a
belief to constitute knowledge is not enough for it to be true; it is
further necessary that there be evidence in its favor, or good reasons
for believing it—or, in any case, that it is not be an arbitrary belief.

JUSTIFICATION: FOUR DISTINCTIONS

What is justification? The first distinction that we need to make is
between properly *epistemic* justification and other kinds of justification. Let us suppose, for instance, that Messi is about to shoot a
free kick. The position of the ball and the quality of the other team

are such that Messi knows that very probably the shot will not be a goal. But if Messi could convince himself that it will be a goal, then the shot will be much better (although it will still not likely be a goal). Many philosophers think that, in this case, Messi is epistemically justified in thinking that he will miss the shot, but he is practically justified in believing that he will make it. This practical justification arises from Messi's objective of scoring a goal: given that believing that he will make the shot raises the probability that he will, forming this belief is the best means available to him to reach this objective. But this practical justification does not translate into epistemic justification: even if he believes it and (by chance) it is true that he will make the shot, he does not know it, nor is he rational in believing it.

There are some philosophers who will dissent from this diagnosis of the case. According to these philosophers, epistemic justification is the only kind of justification that applies to beliefs, while practical justification applies only to actions. These philosophers will say that Messi is practically justified in *trying* to believe that he will make the shot, or in *causing* that belief in himself, but not in having it. Trying to have the belief and causing the belief are actions that Messi can undertake, but believing itself is not an action.

Whether or not epistemic justification is the only kind of justification that applies to beliefs, it is what is in play in the third condition of the tripartite analysis of knowledge. From now on, and unless we say so explicitly, when we talk about justification, we refer to epistemic justification.

Epistemic versus practical justification for beliefs

The practical justification of a belief has to do with the consequences of believing, whereas its epistemic justification does not.

Another important distinction, within epistemic justification, is between *propositional* and *doxastic* justification. The best way of introducing this distinction is by an example. Let us suppose that Messi is amply justified in believing that he will score the penalty he is about to kick. That justification is given in part by Messi's track record in similar situations (which Messi clearly remembers), and in part by considerations regarding his ability (which Messi is aware of). Messi has this justification independently of whether he forms the corresponding belief (to wit, that he will score a goal) or not. This is propositional justification. Subjects have propositional justification for a given proposition if their situation makes them justified in believing that proposition, regardless of whether they *actually* believe it or not. Doxastic justification, by contrast, refers to the justification of the mental state of believing a proposition. To be doxastically justified in believing a proposition is not sufficient to have propositional justification for that proposition and to believe it. If Messi believes that he will score the penalty because he has a temporary delusion of greatness and believes himself infallible, he is not doxastically justified despite having propositional justification for a proposition and believing it. What is needed to be doxastically justified is that the belief in question be properly based on the propositional justification the subject has. What is needed, exactly, for a belief to be properly based is a question about which there is no consensus. Some philosophers think that the answer must make fundamental appeal to the notion of *causation* (the belief must, at least, be caused by the propositional justification the subject has), but other philosophers disagree with these causal theories.

Propositional versus doxastic justification

To have propositional justification for believing a proposition one must have sufficient reasons in favor of that proposition, whether one believes it or not. A belief in a proposition is doxastically justified just in case it is properly based on whatever propositionally justifies it.

In the third place, it is also usual to distinguish between inferential and non-inferential justification (and, hence, knowledge). A belief is (either propositionally or doxastically) inferentially justified if and only if its justification depends on the justification of other belief(s). As we shall see in the second part of this book, at least some versions of Coherentism and Infinitism have it that there are no non-inferentially justified beliefs, but many philosophers do hold that they exist. What can beliefs be justified by, if not other beliefs? As we shall see, one prominent answer is that beliefs can be justified by experience.

Inferential versus non-inferential justification

A belief is inferentially justified if and only if its justification depends on the justification of other beliefs; otherwise, if a belief is justified but not on the basis of other justified beliefs, then it is non-inferentially justified.

We must be careful when applying the distinction between inferential and non-inferential justification, for a belief may in some sense be based on another belief and still be non-inferentially justified. Beliefs whose *content* is about other beliefs may be examples of this category. Suppose, for instance, that for whatever reason Mary believes that she has too many beliefs. This second-order belief of Mary is in one obvious sense based on her first-order beliefs, but it may still count as non-inferentially justified because the content of those first-order beliefs is not relevant to the justification of her second-order belief.

Finally, it is necessary to distinguish also between *prima facie* and *ultima facie* (or *all-things-considered*) justification. This distinction is needed if we hold that justification is *defeasible*. That justification is defeasible means that subjects can be justified in believing a proposition and cease to be so justified by acquiring new information. Thus, for instance, Joe can be justified in believing that he will soon eat and lose this justification once he learns that there is no food in the fridge. Given his initial information, Joe was *prima facie* justified in believing that he was going to eat soon (and, at that time, he also had *ultima facie* justification to so believe), but in learning that there is no food in the fridge he lost that justification.

Defeasibility of justification

A subject can be justified in believing a proposition and lose that justification by acquiring more information.

Prima facie versus ultima facie justification

A subject is *prima facie* justified in believing a proposition just in case he or she has some reasons for believing it. A subject is *ultima facie* justified in believing a proposition just in case he or she has enough *prima facie* justification for believing it and this *prima facie* justification is not defeated.

THEORIES OF JUSTIFICATION: INTERNALISM AND EXTERNALISM

We just distinguished between epistemic and practical justification for believing. But our characterisation of epistemic justification was partly negative and partly vague. The negative part consists in saying that epistemic justification does not involve practical justification to believe, if such a thing exists (and, we can add, neither does it involve moral, or prudential, or some other kind of justification). The vague part consists in saying that epistemic justification is necessary for knowledge. In our defense, it is difficult to go beyond these characterisations without prejudging issues about which epistemologists disagree. In what follows, then, we shall present different *theories* of justification, which are sometimes incompatible with each other.

We will distinguish, to begin with, between two large *kinds* of theories of justification: the internalist and externalist theories. These theories disagree regarding what factors can contribute to the justification of a belief. Internalists hold that these factors must satisfy a certain necessary condition: they must be *internal*, in a sense to be clarified, to the justified subject. On the other hand, any theory which denies any such necessary condition will be an externalist theory.

INTERNALISM VERSUS EXTERNALISM

Internalism: all the factors which justify a proposition for a subject must be internal to that subject.

Externalism: not all the factors which justify a proposition for a subject must be internal to that subject.

So, what is that necessary condition, more precisely? There are at least two kinds of Internalism: *Mentalism* and *Accessibilism*. According to mentalist Internalism, the factors which contribute to the justification of beliefs must be mental states of the subject in question, whereas according to accessibilist Internalism, they must be accessible in a special way to that subject.

MENTALISM AND ACCESSIBILISM

Mentalism: to say that a factor is internal to a subject is to say that it is a mental state of that subject.

Accessibilism: to say that a factor is internal to a subject is to say that it is accessible in a special way by that subject.

A theory can be externalist, then, also in at least two ways: by denying that the factors that contribute to the justification of a belief must be mental states of the subject or by denying that they must be accessible in a special way to the subject. Mentalist Internalism is relatively clear—or, at least, as clear as the very notion of a mental state. But what does it mean to say that the factors that contribute to the justification of beliefs must be accessible to the subject in a special way? What way is that? The idea here is that whereas Sarah may know that Lucy is justified in believing (say) that there is milk in the fridge, the way in which Lucy herself has access to that knowledge (the second-order knowledge that she is justified in believing that there is milk in the fridge) is, first of all, different from the way that Sarah's has access to it, and, in particular, it is more secure. A specific version of accessibilist Mentalism, for instance, holds that the subject whose beliefs are justified has *a priori* access to the very fact that they are justified—whereas, commonly, the kind of access that we have to the justification of other people's beliefs is *a posteriori* (we explain the distinction between *a priori* and *a posteriori* justification later). A subtly different explanation of accessibilism consists in saying that whereas we have introspective access to our own mental states, we do not have introspective access to the mental states of others (where it is left open whether introspection counts as giving us *a priori* knowledge).

Where does the difference between the different kinds of Internalism come from? Accessibilist Internalism has historical priority, and it could be argued that it was assumed, for instance, by Descartes. Mentalist Internalism arose as a reaction to some criticisms of accessibilist Internalism. For instance, one objection to Accessibilism holds that it uncritically inherits the Cartesian thesis of the primacy of self-knowledge, and another objection holds that it is based on an equally uncritical acceptance of the distinction between *a priori* and *a posteriori* knowledge. Faced with these objections, some philosophers prefer to avoid them by setting aside the idea of privileged access but holding that there is nevertheless a *metaphysical* distinction between the justification of one's own beliefs and that of others: what justifies the beliefs of a subject S are S's mental states, whereas what justifies the beliefs of some other subject S★ are the mental states of S★. This mentalist Internalism is sometimes defined as a *supervenience* thesis: two subjects cannot differ regarding the justification of their beliefs without differing regarding their mental states.

AN INTERNALIST THEORY: EVIDENTIALISM

A specific kind of internalist theory, of the mentalist variety, is Evidentialism. According to this view, there are three levels of epistemic justification. The first level concerns objective relations of justification between evidence and doxastic attitudes. The second level is about propositional justification, which holds between a subject and a doxastic attitude just in case that subject's evidence objectively justifies that doxastic attitude. Finally, there is the level of doxastic justification, which results when a subject who has *propositional* justification to form a doxastic attitude does form it based on the evidence which justifies it. It is obvious that the notion of evidence plays a fundamental role in Evidentialism, and so we need to make it more explicit.

Evidentialism

A doxastic attitude of a subject is propositionally justified if and only if it fits the evidence the subject has.

What kinds of things can be evidence? Some philosophers answer that only mental states can be evidence. More specifically, experiences, memories, and doxastic attitudes themselves can function as evidence. Thus, for instance, Joe's experience right now is evidence in favor of believing that he is watching TV, whereas Mary's memories are evidence in favor of suspending judgment regarding the proposition that Bratislava is the Capital of Slovakia. But it is also possible to hold that more complicated mental states can be evidence. For instance, Sarah's logical ability (an ability which, presumably, is a complicated mental state) provides her with evidence in favor of believing that a certain complex proof is valid.

This idea that evidence is constituted exclusively by mental states is not at all the only way of understanding the relation between mental states and evidence. In fact, the insistence on this kind of Mentalism gives rise to complicated questions. To explain one of those issues, let us recall that the logical relation of implication holds between propositions (or sentences, or other truth-bearers). Beliefs, and doxastic attitudes in general (as well as other propositional attitudes), are notably ambiguous between vehicle and content. Thus, for instance, when we speak of Joe's belief, we can refer to a certain mental state of Joe's or to the content of such state—that is to say, a proposition. That is why, despite the fact that the logical relation of implication holds between propositions and not mental states, we can happily say that Joe's belief implies that it is raining—what we mean in that case is that *what Joe believes* (to wit, a certain proposition) implies a certain other proposition (that it is raining). Just as implication (as well as other logical relations) holds between propositions, many philosophers have thought that epistemic relations also hold only between propositions. For these philosophers, it is not correct to say, for instance, that an experience can justify a belief, for the same reason that it is not correct to say that an experience can imply a proposition. But it is not plausible either to hold that experiences have nothing to do with the justification of beliefs. Mary and Sarah both believe that it is raining, but whereas Mary believes it because she is watching the rain, Sarah believes it out of a gloomy disposition. Mary's belief is justified, and Sarah's is not, and it would be extremely implausible to say that that fact has nothing to do with their respective experiences.

If the idea that only propositions can justify other propositions is not to imply that experiences have nothing to do with justification, what does the idea amount to, exactly? Here is a proposal. Let us start by assuming that experiences are themselves propositional attitudes. Thus, for instance, just as we can believe that there is a cat in the garden, we can also have an experience according to which there is a cat in the garden. Even when we assume that experiences have propositional content we must distinguish between experiences and beliefs because it is possible to have an experience according to which a certain proposition is true without believing that proposition (for instance, when faced with the Müller-Lyer illusion, we have an experience according to which the two lines differ in length, but those of us familiar with this optical illusion do not believe that the lines are of different length). The idea, then, is that experiences are relevant to empirical justification not because they are themselves evidence, but rather because they can provide us with evidence. Experiences, according to this conception, are not evidence in favor of their propositional content, but providers of that content as evidence.

The same goes for doxastic attitudes. Mary justifiably believes that it is raining, and based on this she justifiably infers that the picnic will be cancelled. What is Mary's evidence for her belief that the picnic will be cancelled? A strictly mentalist construal of evidence would say that it is Mary's belief that it is raining. But this construal is problematic in a few ways. First, it dangerously ignores the vehicle-content ambiguity regarding belief. Is the evidence Mary's mental state, or its content? And second, assuming that the answer to that first question aligns with a literal reading of Mentalism and holds that it is the very mental state which is the evidence, that seems to misconstrue the bearing of Mary's evidence on the proposition that the picnic will be cancelled. That it is raining is directly relevant to whether the picnic will be cancelled, but whether Mary believes that it is raining is at best indirectly relevant to whether the picnic will be cancelled—it may be relevant, for instance, if Mary is always well-informed about the weather. Better, then, to say that Mary's evidence is that it is raining, and that she has this proposition as evidence in virtue of having a (justified) belief with it as its content. The picture of the role of experiences in justification mirrors what we are saying here about belief: just as beliefs can provide their content as evidence without themselves being evidence, so too experiences can provide their contents as evidence without themselves being evidence.

What are the advantages of this conception of empirical evidence when compared with the first alternative, according to which experiences (and other mental states) are themselves evidence? There are at least two advantages. First, this alternative conception avoids the problems that have to do with saying that *things* (such as experiences and other mental states) can provide evidence for beliefs. Second, this conception also allows for a neater theory of evidence and its possession.

According to this conception, there are also three levels to epistemic justification. The first level is occupied by justification relations among propositions. For instance, the proposition that there is a cat in the garden provides a certain degree of justification to the proposition that there are no birds in the garden (because it is likely that the cat has scared them). This first level exists independently of any subject—objective justification relations among propositions have, in this sense, the same status as relations of logical implication between propositions, which do not depend for their existence on the existence of human beings either.

The second level is that of propositional justification, which does depend on the existence of human beings, for we (or other beings with cognitive capacities which are relevantly similar) are the ones who can have or lack propositional justification for believing propositions. Thus, if Joe has an experience whose propositional content is that there is a cat in the garden, then generally that experience provides Joe with the proposition that there is a cat in the garden as evidence, and then Joe has a certain degree of propositional justification for believing that there are no birds in the garden.

Finally, the third level is that of doxastic justification, which requires not just propositional justification but also appropriate basing of doxastic attitudes on the evidence which justifies them. We should add that when subjects have an experience with a certain propositional content (and the situation is otherwise normal), then they have justification for forming not only those doxastic attitudes that are objectively justified by the proposition that is the content of the experience but also for believing that proposition itself. In our example, the subject is justified in believing not only that there are no birds in the garden but also that there is a cat in the garden. We can, if we want, even say that what justifies the subject in believing that there is a cat in the garden is his experience. But we must distinguish this kind of justification by experience from the evidential justification that exists between his belief that there is a cat in the garden and his belief that there are no birds in the garden. The subject's evidence is that there is a cat in the garden, and this evidence justifies him in believing that there are no birds in the garden. Of course, the subject is also justified in believing that there is a cat in the garden, but that justification is not based on any evidence. We can say that the subject has no evidence in favor of the proposition that there is a cat in the garden, if we do not take that to mean that his belief is arbitrary. On the contrary, his belief is perfectly well justified, but not by evidence. To say that the experience itself is the evidence is to go back to the mentalist theory of evidence.

Why not go back to this mentalist theory of evidence? We already mentioned one reason: because it gets tangled up in the question of how it can be that a thing (an experience, for instance) provides evidence for a doxastic attitude. And we were in the middle of explaining another reason. We said that it is relatively clear what are the connections between the three levels of justification according to the alternative theory of evidence. How are those connections explained according to Mentalism? According to that theory, there is no clear distinction between the first and the second level. The first level already includes mental states such as experiences and beliefs. If experiences themselves are evidence, for instance, it does not make sense to distinguish between evidence and its possession. The experience as of a cat in the garden justifies Mary in believing that there are no birds in the garden as long as that experience is had *by Mary*. That Joe has such an experience tells us nothing regarding which doxastic attitudes are justified for Mary. The level of objective justification, then, already must mention subjects. It is neater, we believe, to make a clear distinction between objective relations of justification among propositions and the possession of some of those propositions as evidence.

MENTALISM VERSUS PROPOSITIONALISM ABOUT EVIDENCE

Mentalism: the evidence a subject S has is constituted by S's mental states, such as (some of) S's beliefs and S's experiences.

Propositionalism: the evidence a subject S has is constituted by propositions which are the contents of S's mental states, such as the content of (some of) S's beliefs and experiences.

Whichever one of those two theories of evidence we adopt, Evidentialism will be an internalist theory, for it will respect the supervenience of justification on mental states: there cannot be two subjects that differ with respect to which doxastic attitudes they are justified in having without differing in their mental states.

Let us now consider the most common objections to Evidentialism. In the first place, it is notable that Evidentialism (at least in its most famous versions) is a *non-reductive* theory of justification. By this, we mean that it explains epistemic justification in terms of the notion of fittingness with evidence, and this latter is itself an epistemic notion. As a result, Evidentialism appeals to primitive epistemic notions. Some philosophers will be uncomfortable with a theory with an epistemic primitive. For those philosophers, then, Evidentialism is not acceptable (at least not without additions to the theory).

Another objection to Evidentialism attacks the central idea of the theory: that justification depends on evidence. Some philosophers hold that there is justification without evidence—for instance, our justification for believing that our basic processes of belief formation produce justified beliefs cannot itself rest on evidence on pains of vicious circularity, according to these philosophers. We will examine a version of this proposal in the second part of the book.

AN EXTERNALIST THEORY: RELIABILISM

We said before that a theory is considered externalist simply in virtue of denying that all of the factors that determine the justification of beliefs are internal (in any of the senses we distinguished: mental states of the subject or states to which the subject has some form of privileged access). In this section, we introduce one of the most influential externalist theories in contemporary epistemology: Reliabilism.

According to a mad-dog version of Reliabilism (which, as we shall soon see, has not actually been suggested by anyone), a belief is justified if and only if it is produced by a reliable belief-forming process. What does it mean to say that a belief-forming process is reliable? To a first approximation, it means that it produces more true than false beliefs. Thus, for example, let us consider vision under normal conditions as a method of belief formation. At least on its face (as we will see later there are reasons to doubt what follows), it is reasonable to think that that process is reliable, for, despite the existence of visual illusions, they are not statistically significative. According to this version of Reliabilism, then, the beliefs produced by that process are justified. Notice that Evidentialism and Reliabilism have something in common: according to both theories, there can be justified beliefs that are false. For there can be *misleading* evidence: for instance, you may have very good evidence that it will rain today (say, in the form of a weather forecast with a 90% probability of rain) even though it will not. In that case, according to Evidentialism, you are justified in believing that it will rain. And there can also be justified false beliefs according to Reliabilism, for the processes need not be *perfectly* reliable to produce justification. Thus, Mary's belief that there is a puddle of water down the road may be justified even when it is false, for it is produced by a process (namely, visual perception) that produces more true than false beliefs—even though it did produce a false belief in this case.

It is clear, then, why Reliabilism counts as an externalist theory: the fact that vision is a reliable process of belief formation is neither a mental state nor accessible in any special way to the subjects that use it.

Now, why did we say that that version of Reliabilism is a mad-dog version that no one endorses? In the first place, because it ignores inferential justification. Let us suppose, for instance, that Jane is justified in believing that the car keys are on the table (she left them there five minutes ago), but that, unbeknownst to Jane, Bob took them from the table and put them in his pocket. Based in part on her belief that the car keys are on the table, Jane infers that she will be driving in five minutes. Is Jane justified in believing this? We would say that she is: given that she is justified in believing that she will easily find the keys, she is also justified in believing that she will soon be driving, despite the fact that both of these beliefs are false (and, therefore, despite the fact that she does not know either of these propositions). Reliabilism, then, should deliver the result that Jane is justified in believing that she will soon be driving. But our mad-dog formulation of Reliabilism has the opposite result. The process of inferring based on false beliefs is not reliable—it produces as many false as true beliefs. The problem, as we said, resides in the fact that the mad-dog version of Reliabilism does not consider inferential justification.

To solve this issue, we can appeal to a recursive definition of justification. We explained what a recursive definition is when we discussed the correspondence theory of truth. Applied to

Reliabilism, we can solve the problem of inferential justification by appealing to the following recursive definition (notice that the "only if" part of the definition takes the place of the closure clause):

RELIABILIST DEFINITION OF JUSTIFICATION

S is justified in believing that p if and only if:

Base clause: S's belief that p is formed by a belief-independent belief-forming process, and that process is reliable; or

Recursive clause: S's belief that p is formed by a belief-dependent process that is conditionally reliable, and S is justified in believing each of the propositions on which the process depends.

This definition is remarkable not only because of its recursive structure but also because it appeals, in its second clause, to the notion of *conditional reliability*. We said before that the basic idea of a reliable belief-forming process is that it produces more true than false beliefs. A process that depends on other beliefs is conditionally reliable if and only if it produces more true than false beliefs under the assumption that the beliefs on which it depends are themselves true. Notice that this does not mean that to be inferentially justified it is necessary that the beliefs on which the process depends (the beliefs which form the basis of the inference) *be* true—all that is needed, roughly put, is that if they *were* true then the process would produce more true than false beliefs.

A problem with that Reliabilist definition of justification has to do with the defeasibility of justification. Let us suppose that Anne opens her eyes and has an experience as of a red wall in front of her. In that case, she is *prima facie* justified in believing that the wall is red, and Reliabilism has no problem delivering that verdict. But let us suppose that Anne now learns that there are red lights shining on the wall (which means that the wall would look red even if it is white). Given this new information, Anne loses her *ultima facie* justification for believing that the wall is red. But how can Reliabilism deliver this result? A possible solution to this problem, which we will not analyze here in detail, is that the recursive reliabilist definition of justification is a definition of *prima facie* justification, and that this justification becomes *ultima facie* only if subjects do not have available other reliable processes such that, if they were to base their beliefs on them, then their beliefs would not be justified. The basic thought is to capture the very idea of defeaters in reliabilist terms.

From the point of view of its proponents, Reliabilism is significant not only because of its externalist character but also because it gives us a characterisation of epistemic justification in non-epistemic terms. To understand what we mean by this, let us go back to Evidentialism. According to this theory, a belief is justified for a subject just in case the subject has sufficient evidence for it. Now, as we said when discussing Evidentialism, the very idea of evidence in favor of a belief is epistemic—the project of deciding which mental states (or which propositions, depending on the kind of Evidentialism we favor) are evidence for which beliefs is a paradigmatically epistemic project. If Evidentialism does not say anything else about that project (and their most famous defenders typically do not say much else), then it is a theory that rests on an epistemic primitive. Reliabilism, by contrast, defines justification in terms of the reliability of belief-forming processes, a clearly non-epistemic notion. Reliabilism, then, promises to be a reductive theory of justification.

Let us now turn to the most important objections to Reliabilism. In explaining these objections, we will concentrate on the rough version of Reliabilism according to which the reliability of the belief-forming process is necessary and sufficient for justification. We set aside the subtleties needed for Reliabilism to account for inferential justification and the defeasibility of justification because the objections do not concern those subtleties.

A first objection holds that reliability is not sufficient for justification. A by-now famous fictional case is that of a subject who, unbeknownst to himself, has partial clairvoyance. In particular, this subject has spontaneous beliefs about the whereabouts of the president, and those beliefs are almost always true. It is important to stipulate that the subject has not had time to mount an argument in favor of the reliability of those spontaneous beliefs—let us suppose, for instance, that he has just started to have these beliefs, and that he has not verified them. We need to make some such supposition because what we want to determine is whether reliability by itself is sufficient for justification, not whether information about the reliability of some process is sufficient. Even a staunch Evidentialist would agree that that if someone knows that their beliefs were produced by a reliable process, then they have evidence in favor of those beliefs—and so they are justified. The question, then, is not whether someone who knows that they are clairvoyant (or knows in some other way that their beliefs are produced by reliable processes) has justified beliefs, but rather whether reliability by itself can generate justified beliefs. And the idea of the case in question is that the answer has to be negative. When the subject suddenly believes that the president is in Paris, that belief is not justified, even if it was produced by a reliable belief-forming process.

How successful is this objection to Reliabilism? The question is complicated precisely because of what we just mentioned: we cannot suppose that the subject knows that he is clairvoyant, and we cannot suppose either that he knows that most of his beliefs about the whereabouts of the president are true. Otherwise, we would be testing not whether reliability by itself is sufficient for justification, but rather whether information about reliability is so sufficient. But if we take that stipulation seriously, then it would seem as if the subject has a defeater for his belief that the president is in Paris. That defeater is the following: my belief that the president is in Paris is not based on any grounds for thinking that the president is in Paris. The reliabilist can then say that the belief is indeed not justified, but not because reliability cannot generate justification, but rather because it generates *prima facie* justification which in this case is defeated.

One could try to create counterexamples to the sufficiency of reliability for justification which do not have that problem with defeasibility (at least not in an obvious way). Some people know which leaves correspond to which kind of tree. Thus, if they see a spirally arranged leaf with lobate margins, they know that it is most likely an oak leaf. Let us suppose that a subject is born, not with clairvoyance, but rather with an automatic belief-forming mechanism that makes her believe that leaves with those characteristics are oak leaves. It can be argued that this subject does not have defeaters for her beliefs, for she can say what they are based on: on the phenotypical characteristics of the leaves. However, if the subject did not learn in the ordinary way to identify oak leaves, but rather was lucky to be born with that automatic mechanism, then it is difficult to say that the corresponding beliefs are justified. One could also argue, however, that the very fact that the subject did not learn to identify oak leaves in the ordinary way is something that the subject knows, and that very information can function as a defeater.

A second objection to Reliabilism attacks the necessity of reliability for justification. In the second part of this book, we will examine *skeptical scenarios* in detail, but we will now introduce the basic idea. A skeptical scenario is a hypothesis according to which most of the beliefs of the subject in question are false (or, in other variants, true but unknown to the subject for other reasons), but the subject cannot distinguish his case from the normal one. For instance, Descartes' evil demon, which deceives a disembodied soul into believing that he is a normal human being, is a skeptical scenario, as is also the supposition that we are connected to a computer that stimulates our brain to make us have the same experiences that a normal subject would have. As we said, we will study the use of these scenarios as arguments in favor of skepticism in the second part of this book. For now, we are interested in the subjects who are the protagonists of these skeptical scenarios. Those subjects cannot have knowledge by construction of the cases, but an interesting question is whether they can have justified beliefs. And the answer seems to be obviously affirmative: if those subjects form their beliefs in the normal way (for instance, if they take their experiences at face value), then they will be fully justified despite lacking knowledge. For instance, when a character in the movie *The Matrix* believes that she is eating ice cream, that belief is justified (despite the fact that it does not constitute knowledge because she is not, in fact, eating ice cream). But notice that the process that formed that belief (to wit, the process consisting in taking experience at face value) is not at all reliable. The vast majority of the beliefs which result from this process are false. Therefore, the argument goes, a belief can be justified even if the process that created it is not reliable. In other words, reliability is not necessary for justification. This objection has come to be known as the "new evil demon" objection to Reliabilism.

The clairvoyant's case attacks the sufficiency of reliability for justification, whereas consideration of skeptical scenarios attacks its necessity. Both objections presuppose that the notion of reliability itself is intelligible (otherwise they could not argue that it is not sufficient or necessary for justification). The third (and last) objection that we will consider attacks precisely this supposition. According to the "generality problem" (as this objection has been called), the very notion of reliability suffers from a kind of vagueness that makes it inapplicable.

Let us start by observing that, at least in principle, reliability is a property of *types* of processes, not of token processes. This is so because a token process generates one and only one belief, which means that no meaningful degree of reliability can be assigned to it—if the belief it generated is true, then it is perfectly reliable, whereas if the belief it generated is false it is perfectly unreliable, and adopting these degrees would collapse the distinction between justified and true belief. To generate meaningful degrees of reliability, then, we must concentrate not on the particular token process which generated the beliefs, but rather on the general type of process (the type *visual process*, for instance). But (and this is the core of the problem) any token process belongs to indefinitely many types of processes. For instance, let us suppose that Bob wakes up one morning, puts his glasses on, takes a glance out the window, and as a result believes that it is raining. The token process that generated Bob's belief belongs to an indefinite number of types of processes, including the following: visual process, visual process aided by glasses, visual process aided by glasses taking place in a teenager, process which takes place in the morning, process that creates beliefs about the weather, process consisting in looking through a window, process which takes place in a subject wearing socks, etc. Each one of these types of processes will have its own degree of reliability, which need not coincide with the degree of the other types. The question underlying the generality problem is then the following: which of the types of processes under which any token process falls is relevant to the evaluation of reliability? Intuitively, some of the processes we mentioned are more relevant than others: for instance, in general, it does not matter if the subject was using socks or not, but it does matter whether the subject used glasses. But the problem consists in formulating general principles that allow us to determine, given any case of belief formation, which type of process to use to assess its reliability.

Needless to say, philosophers have formulated answers to these problems for Reliabilism. But it is not our intention to get here into the details of these answers, but rather to delineate the main areas in which a reliabilist would have to work to have a defensible theory.

SUMMARY

In this chapter, we have provided a preliminary examination of the tripartite conception of propositional knowledge. According to that conception, knowledge is justified true belief. We examined each of the concepts involved in that definition: truth, belief, and justification. Regarding truth, we discussed the three classical theories—truth as correspondence, truth as coherence, and the pragmatist conception of truth—as well as the more contemporary deflationary approach. We explained the place of belief as a kind of doxastic attitude—and, therefore, a kind of mental state. Finally, we made several distinctions regarding justification, and we examined two of the main theories of justification available in the contemporary literature: Evidentialism and Reliabilism. In the next chapter, we continue our examination of the tripartite conception of propositional knowledge with the main objection that has been levelled against it.

FURTHER READING

A synthesis of Evidentialism and Reliabilism is proposed in Juan Comesaña, "Evidentialist Reliabilism", *Noûs* 44 (2010), pp. 571–600.

A thorough discussion of theories of truth can be found in Michael Glanzberg, "Truth", in Edward N. Zalta (ed.), *The Stanford Encyclopedia of Philosophy* (Fall 2018 edition), https://plato.stanford.edu/archives/fall2018/entries/truth/.

For a canonical defense of Evidentialism, see Richard Feldman and Earl Conee, "Internalism Defended", *American Philosophical Quarterly* 38(1) (2001), pp. 1–18.

For a comprehensive discussion of propositions, see Matthew McGrath and Devin Frank, "Propositions", in Edward N. Zalta (ed.), *The Stanford Encyclopedia of Philosophy* (Winter 2020 edition), https://plato.stanford.edu/archives/win2020/entries/propositions/.

For an encyclopedic introduction to the issues of this and the following chapter, see Jonathan Ichikawa and Matthias Steup, "The Analysis of Knowledge", in Edward N. Zalta (ed.), *The Stanford Encyclopedia of Philosophy* (Summer 2018 edition), https://plato.stanford.edu/archives/sum2018/entries/knowledge-analysis/.

For the classical statement of Reliabilism, see Alvin Goldman, "What Is Justified Belief?", in G. S. Pappas (ed.), *Justification and Knowledge* (1979), Reidel, pp. 1–25.

The clairvoyant objection to Reliabilism is from Laurence BonJour, "Externalist Theories of Empirical Knowledge", *Midwest Studies in Epistemology* V (1980), pp. 53–73.

The generality problem for Reliabilism was already recognized by Goldman in the paper cited earlier, and is forcefully pressed by Earl Conee and Richard Feldman, "The Generality Problem", *Philosophical Studies* 89 (1998), pp. 1–29. For a reply, see, for example, Juan Comesaña, "A Well-Founded Solution to the Generality Problem", *Philosophical Studies* 129 (2006), pp. 127–147.

The new evil demon objection to Reliabilism appeared originally in Stew Cohen, "Justification and Truth", *Philosophical Studies* 46 (1984), pp. 279–295.

THE GETTIER PROBLEM

INTRODUCTION

We turn now to one of the most influential episodes in the contemporary theory of knowledge: the critique of the traditional
definition due to the American philosopher Edmund Gettier. This
critique gave rise to the so-called "Gettier problem": the problem
of trying to fix the traditional definition in light of Gettier's critique.
We will examine a couple of such proposed fixes, but both of them
have serious problems. Moreover, this is not simply a feature of the
particular theories that we chose the concentrate on, but a more
general phenomenon: there simply is no consensus on the philosophical literature on how to answer the Gettier problem. This gives
rise to a meta-problem (which has been called "the Gettier problem
problem"): why is this so? That is to say, why is there no generally
accepted answer to the Gettier problem? Examining this question
will lead us to the work of another famous American Philosopher,
Willard Van Orman Quine, who argued against the idea that it is
possible to give informative definitions of interesting philosophical
concepts. If Quine is right, then we have an answer to the Gettier problem problem: there is no generally accepted answer to the
Gettier problem simply because there is no informative definition
of propositional knowledge to be had. A more moderate version
of this position can be gleaned from the contemporary program
of "knowledge-first epistemology," according to which the notion
of propositional knowledge is itself basic, and so cannot be defined
in simpler terms. We end the chapter with a brief discussion of this
influential contemporary position in epistemology.

DOI: 10.4324/9781003208440-5

GETTIER'S ARGUMENT

Recall the tripartite definition of propositional knowledge:

THE TRIPARTITE CONCEPTION OF KNOWLEDGE

S knows that p if and only if:

1. p is true;
2. S believes that p;
3. S is justified in believing that p.

The three conditions, we said, are treated by the tripartite conception as individually necessary and jointly sufficient for propositional knowledge. To say that they are individually necessary is to say that each one of them must be satisfied if the subject is to know the proposition, and to say that they are collectively sufficient is to say that if all of them are satisfied, then the subject knows the proposition. Thus, proponents of the tripartite conception are saying that justified true belief is to knowledge what female fox is to vixen.

Remember also that there are two ways in which a proposed definition such as that one can go wrong: the conditions may fail to be individually necessary, or they may fail to be jointly sufficient—and, of course, both defects can be had at the same time. Here are examples of those failures:

DEFECTIVE DEFINITION OF DOG (UNNECESSARY)

X is a dog if and only if:
1. X is a Basenji.

DEFECTIVE DEFINITION OF DOG (INSUFFICIENT)

X is a dog if and only if:
1. X is a mammal.

DEFECTIVE DEFINITION OF DOG (UNNECESSARY AND INSUFFICIENT)

X is a dog if and only if:
1. X is a hairless animal.

Gettier argued that the tripartite conception of knowledge exhibits the second of these defects—that is to say, he argued that justified true belief is insufficient for knowledge. He argued for this both directly and indirectly. He argued directly by providing examples of cases where a subject has a justified true belief but does not have knowledge. And he argued indirectly by providing a recipe for anyone to generate more examples like that.

Let us start with the cases. For his first case, let us suppose that two subjects, say Mary and Jeff, have applied for the same job. Let us also suppose that Mary has strong (though not conclusive) evidence for believing the following conjunctive proposition: (a) Jeff will get the job and he has ten coins in his pocket. Let us suppose, for instance, that Mary has just counted the coins in Jeff's pocket, and knows that he is the preferred candidate for the job. Proposition (a) implies the following proposition (b): whoever will get the job has ten coins in his or her pocket. Mary sees that (a) implies (b) and on that basis believes (b). Finally, let us suppose that, unbeknownst to Mary, it is she who will get the job, and she also has ten coins in her pocket. Gettier claims that Mary then has a justified true belief in (b) but does not know that (b) is true.

Gettier's second case, slightly modified, is the following. Let us suppose that Mary and Jeff work in the same office. Jeff likes Ford cars very much, and he lets this be known to his co-workers. Jeff says that he owns a Ford, and Mary has seen him many times driving a Ford. On the basis of that evidence, Mary believes (c) that Jeff owns a Ford. And, on the basis of her belief in (c), Mary deduces (and comes to believe) (d) that a co-worker owns a Ford. Now, Jeff is actually lying, and does not own a Ford. Unbeknownst to Mary, however, someone else in the office does own a Ford. Therefore, Mary has a justified true belief in (d) that, according to Gettier, does not amount to knowledge.

Let us now turn to Gettier's recipe for generating this kind of cases. The recipe rests on two assumptions: that it is possible to have justified false beliefs, and that one can be justified in believing what follows logically from what one is already justified in believing:

False justified beliefs are possible: It is possible to be justified in believing a false proposition.

Closure principle for justification: If S is justified in believing that p, and p implies q, and S deduces q from p and accepts q as a result of that deduction, then S is justified in believing q.

The closure principle deserves a couple of clarifications. First of all, why is it called a "closure" principle? The terminology is mathematical. The idea is that some sets can be defined by specifying some of its members and then stipulating that anything else that bears some specified relation to those initial members is also a member. Thus, for instance, the set of natural numbers can be specified as the set that contains the number 0 (or 1, depending on where you like to start counting) and is "closed" under the operation of adding 1 (or the successor operation). In the case of the closure principle for justification, what it says (roughly speaking) is that the set of justified beliefs is closed under the operation of logical implication. The second clarification regarding the closure principle, then, has to do precisely with this idea: what does it mean to say a proposition logically implies another? For our purposes here, the following definition will suffice:

Logical entailment: A proposition p logically entails (or implies) another proposition q if and only if it is impossible for p to be true and q false at the same time.

There are different notions of possibility. Some of them are relative: it is not possible, given the laws of physics, for anything to accelerate past the speed of light; it is not possible, given the present state of technology, to have a cell-phone battery that lasts 10,000 hours without needing to be recharged. The first one is an impossibility relative to the laws of physics and the second one an impossibility relative to the current state of our technology. But neither of them is impossible in an absolute sense: there is no inconsistency in supposing that we can have cell-phone batteries that last 10,000 hours—we just have to assume that our technology has advanced a lot. Similarly, there is no inconsistency in supposing that a rocket accelerates beyond the speed of light—we just have to assume that the laws of physics are different from what we currently take them to be. It is this latter, absolute notion of possibility, that is involved in the definition of logical entailment.

With those clarifications made, notice that both of the theories of justification we examined in the previous chapter seem to validate both of these assumptions. Take Evidentialism first. It seems perfectly possible to have evidence for a belief that falls short of entailing that the belief is true, and so Evidentialism seems compatible with the assumption that it is possible to have false justified beliefs. We will see in Chapter 5 that there is a lot more to say about closure principles, but meanwhile it also seems perfectly possible for one's evidence for a proposition p to also be evidence for a proposition q that is entailed by p, and so it looks like Evidentialism also validates the closure principle. Take now Reliabilism. Reliabilism is tailor-made to satisfy the assumption that we can have false justified beliefs, for it is part and parcel of Reliabilism that perfect reliability is not necessary for justification. Moreover, the recursive structure of the definition of Reliabilism in the previous chapter guarantees that a Reliabilist theory will satisfy closure—if p entails q, then the conditional reliability of q given p is as high as it can be.

On the basis of those suppositions, Gettier's recipe to formulate counterexamples to the tripartite conception of propositional knowledge is the following (Gettier himself does not explicitly formulate the recipe in his note):

Gettier's recipe: Start by describing a case where a subject S is justified in believing a certain false proposition p (that this is possible is guaranteed by the first assumption). Then make S believe another proposition q on the basis of deducing it from p. The second assumption guarantees that S is also justified in believing q. Lastly, end the description of the case by making sure that q is true. Given that p is false, the truth of q cannot be due to the truth of p. S's belief in q is true, but fortuitously so. Thus, S has a true justified belief in q, but does not know that q is true, thus refuting the tripartite conception of knowledge.

As you can verify, Gettier's own cases fit this recipe. In the first one, p is the proposition that Jeff will get the job and he has ten coins in his pocket and q is the proposition that whoever will get the job has ten coins in his or her pocket. In the second one, p is the proposition that Jeff owns a Ford and q is the proposition that a co-worker owns a Ford.

Something interesting about Gettier cases is that they involve two strokes of luck: one stroke of bad luck and one stroke of good luck. The stroke of bad luck is that the initial belief *p* is false, whereas the stroke of good luck is that the target belief *q* is nevertheless true. In this respect, Gettier cases (which are about justified belief and knowledge) can be compared with cases of lucky action. Suppose, for instance, that a golfer strikes the ball competently, in such a way that the shot would have been very good in normal circumstances. However, a bird catches the ball in the air and flies away with it. By chance, the bird releases the ball right above the hole, resulting in a hole-in-one. The golfer also had two strokes of luck: bad luck in that the bird stole his good shot; good luck in that the bird released the ball at the best possible moment. We can now compare our reactions to the golfer with our reactions to the protagonists of Gettier cases. Many of us would at least hesitate before attributing the hole-in-one to the golfer, even if he would have gotten it anyway had the bird not intervened. (The official rules of golf seem to agree: rule 19–1 (a) appears to indicate that the ball must be dropped as close as possible to where the bird first caught it.) That analogy might illuminate why many of us similarly are at the very least hesitant to attribute knowledge in Gettier cases: just as the hole-in-one is not properly attributable to the player, the true belief is not properly attributable to the subject, and hence does not count as knowledge.

GETTIER'S PROBLEM

There are many possible reactions to Gettier's argument. Let us first think about ways one could reject that argument. One could, for instance, deny one of the assumptions on which it rests. Thus, one could hold an *infallibilist* theory of justification, according to which it is not possible to be justified in believing a false proposition:

Infallibilism about justification: It is not possible to be justified in believing a false proposition.

One could also reject the other assumption of Gettier's argument, the closure principle. As we already anticipated, we will study closure in more detail in Chapter 5. Finally, one could reject Gettier's argument by denying that the subjects in question do not have knowledge.

All of those reactions to Gettier's argument are possible, but what is by far the most common reaction is to agree with Gettier that the tripartite conception of propositional knowledge is wrong because justified true belief is not sufficient for knowledge. Those who thus agree with Gettier must face now the problem of how to fix that conception. This is what we will call "the Gettier problem." There are at least two ways of approaching the Gettier problem. We can, first, hold that the tripartite conception of propositional knowledge is merely incomplete: that, despite the fact that Gettier has shown that justified true belief is not sufficient for knowledge, each one of those three conditions is necessary, and that it is possible to fix the tripartite conception simply by finding a fourth condition that restores sufficiency. This strategy leads to the search for the fourth condition for propositional knowledge. In the second place, we can hold that Gettier showed not only that justified true belief is not sufficient for knowledge but more fundamentally that the tripartite conception starts from an incorrect foundation. The solution to Gettier's problem, according to this second way of approaching it, consists not in finding a fourth condition, but in finding an adequate replacement for the justification condition. We consider next examples of these two strategies.

IN SEARCH OF THE FOURTH CONDITION: NO FALSE LEMMAS

We just said that one way of rejecting Gettier's argument consists in embracing infallibilism about justification and holding that we cannot be justified in believing false propositions. But there is a view that is not infallibilist about justification, because it allows that we can be justified in believing false propositions, but does hold that we cannot have knowledge by inferring from a false proposition. Such a view has it that although Mary is justified in believing both p (Jeff will get the job and he has ten coins in his pocket) and q (whoever will get the job has ten coins in his or her pocket), she does not know q because she infers it from p and p is false. Because p functions somewhat like a lemma does in mathematical proofs (i.e., it is not the target proposition we are ultimately interested in, but it is an important component of our proof of that target proposition), this view is sometimes called the "no false lemmas" view:

No false lemmas: S knows that p if and only if:

1. p is true;
2. S believes that p;
3. S is justified in believing that p;
4. S's belief that p is not based on any falsehood.

We saw what the no false lemmas view would say about one of the original Gettier cases. You can figure out for yourself what it would say about the other one we examined. In general, following Gettier's recipe for generating counterexamples to the tripartite conception means that the case in question will violate the fourth condition of the no false lemmas view.

But there are other cases, which, despite not following Gettier's recipe to the letter, nevertheless are also routinely classified as "Gettier cases" and which seem to cause trouble to the no false lemmas view as much as to the tripartite conception of propositional knowledge. We will briefly describe three such cases.

Consider first the following case (named after its creator, Bertrand Russell, who did not think of it as a counterexample to the tripartite conception of knowledge):

Russell's clock: Julia takes a casual glance at the clock on the wall, which says it is 2:55, and on that basis comes to believe that it is 2:55. Unbeknownst to Julia, the clock has stopped working a while ago, but, coincidentally, it happens to be 2:55.

Notice first that while **Russell's clock** has some of the marks of a typical Gettier case, it arguably does not have them all. It does have the "double luck" structure that we commented on earlier: Julia has a stroke of bad luck in that, unbeknownst to her, the clock has stopped working, but she also has a stroke of good luck in looking at the clock at precisely the right time. However, this double luck takes a slightly different form in Russell's clock than in the original Gettier cases. In the original Gettier cases, the stroke of bad luck consists in the falsity of the initial belief *p*. But Julia arguably does not have two beliefs in this case: she simply believes that it is 2:55 based on her glance at the clock. If we agree with this description of the case and also think that Julia does not know that it is 2:55, then the case represents a counter-example not only to the tripartite conception of knowledge but to the no false lemmas view as well: Julia has a justified true belief that it is 2:55, does not know it, and this belief is not based on any falsehood. The defender of the no false lemmas view could, of course, still argue that there is at least an *implicit* false belief about the functioning of the clock, and that in the absence of that belief the belief about the time would not be justified. The adjudication of this dispute requires a detailed discussion about the distinction between implicit and explicit beliefs and its epistemic relevance, a discussion which we will not carry on here (but which we will mention again in our discussion of Infinitism in the second part of this book).

Our second case is also named after its author Roderick Chisholm, who did very much think of it as a Gettier-style case:

Chisholm's sheep: Joe is looking at a hill and sees what he takes to be a sheep. Actually, what Joe sees is a dog that looks like a sheep from Joe's perspective. Unbeknownst to Joe, there is a sheep hidden behind the dog.

In this case, we are invited to think that Joe has a justified true belief that there is a sheep in the field, and that this belief is not based on any other belief of Joe's but is simply the result of taking what he sees at face value. Here too the defender of the no false lemmas view could object to this last point, and insist that there is a false belief of Joe's that is playing a crucial role in supporting his belief that there is a sheep in the field—perhaps the belief that Joe would express by saying while pointing at the dog: "*That* thing over there is a sheep." As with Russell's clock, the dispute therefore rests on whether any subject in Joe's situation must have some such belief—the defender of the no false lemmas view has to insist that they do.

Finally, let us consider yet another famous case, named again after its author (who, this time, thought of it as a counterexample to the causal theory of knowledge to be examined later):

Ginet's barns: The inhabitants of a Midwest city decide to feign prosperity by peppering the countryside with many fake barns. These "barns" are actually mere barn facades with nothing behind them. Nevertheless, from the highway, they cannot be distinguished from real barns. Let us suppose that Sue is driving on the highway in the area and that she fixes her gaze in the only real barn around, surrounded by fake barns, and comes to believe that there is a (real) barn by the side of the road.

The idea of **Ginet's barns** is that Sue does not know that what she sees is a barn, despite having a justified true belief. Can the defender of the no false lemmas view deploy the same maneuver as in the previous two cases, claiming that Sue's true belief that there is a barn by the side of the road is based on some other false belief of hers? In this case, that strategy is harder to implement. Notice, for instance, that even if Sue has a belief that she would express by saying, while pointing at the barn that she is seeing, "*That* is a barn," this belief is true. Depending on how the case is developed, Mary may well have some false beliefs. For instance, she may believe that all the barns in the area are real barns. But two things are worth noting: first, the case can also be developed so that Mary *does not* have any of those beliefs (she just happened to see only the real barn, for instance); second, even if she does have those false beliefs, her true belief about the real barn is not inferred from them.

If any of those three cases are cases where the subject has a justified true belief not based on a falsehood which does not amount to knowledge, then the no false lemmas view fails in the same way in which the tripartite conception of knowledge failed: its conditions are not sufficient for propositional knowledge. This does not mean that the no false lemmas view is an obvious dead end, in part because (as we shall see later) there are reasons to believe that there are all sorts of background conditions at play in belief formation. But at the very least the burden is on the no false lemmas theorist to explain exactly how their view accounts for the examples given earlier.

There are also other cases which suggest that the no false lemmas theory fails also in the other direction. In particular, some philosophers have argued that it is possible to have knowledge on the basis of false beliefs. Here we will simply mention some of the cases that allegedly show that, leaving their evaluation to the reader. First case: Ann believes that Santa Claus will leave presents under the Christmas tree. On the basis of that belief, Anne believes that there will be presents under the tree, and that belief constitutes knowledge. Second case: Isaac believes in the literal truth of Newton's theory (as Einstein showed, Newton's theory is only an approximation to the truth). On the basis of that belief, Isaac infers that it is possible to send a spaceship to the moon, and that belief amounts to knowledge. Third case: Bertrand believes that it is ten past nine—but his watch is running somewhat fast and it is actually only eight past nine. On the basis of his belief, Bertrand infers that he will not be late for his ten-thirty meeting, and that belief amounts to knowledge.

The no false lemmas theory was one of the first attempts to solve the Gettier problem. The history of Anglo-American epistemology in the twenty years since the publication of Gettier's note until the mid-80s is largely the history of more and more complicated proposals for the fourth condition for propositional knowledge, followed almost immediately by more and more complicated counterexamples to those proposals. It goes perhaps without saying that there is no consensus regarding which fourth condition theory could be the correct one. On the contrary, the majority of philosophers working on the subject believe that no such theory has solved the Gettier problem. Perhaps a different way of tackling the Gettier problem has a better chance of succeeding?

THE REPLACEMENT OF THE JUSTIFICATION CONDITION

Let us recall that at least one intuition that underlies the acceptance of Gettier cases as counterexamples to the tripartite conception of propositional knowledge is that the subjects in those cases are lucky to have true beliefs. Let us also recall that the inclusion of the justification condition in the tripartite conception is based, in general, on the idea that a mere true belief cannot amount to knowledge because its truth can be due to mere luck. Thus, the inclusion of the justification condition was supposed to exclude the possibility that the truth of belief was due to such luck. Gettier cases show that this luck can actually coexist with justification, but not with knowledge.

The search for a fourth condition as a strategy to solve the Gettier problem can be understood as an attempt to get rid of the possibility of that kind of luck once and for all. Faced with the failure of those attempts, some philosophers have concluded that the way to exclude that kind of luck is not with a fourth condition, but rather by replacing the justification condition with some other condition that can correctly do the job that the justification condition was unable to perform.

Some of these philosophers have proposed a version of Reliabilism, not as a theory of justification, but as the third condition in a modified tripartite conception of propositional knowledge:

RELIABILIST THEORY OF KNOWLEDGE

S knows that p if and only if:

1. S believes that p;
2. p is true;
3. S's belief that p was produced by a reliable belief-forming process.

Reliabilism about knowledge will inherit some of the problems of Reliabilism about justification. For instance, if the clairvoyant case shows that reliability is not sufficient for justification, that would be a reason to think that it is not sufficient for knowledge either: if the clairvoyant is not justified, then he does not have knowledge either. The generality problem applies as much to Reliabilism about knowledge as it does to Reliabilism about justification. The new evil demon problem is an exception: Reliabilism about knowledge has the consequence that victims of an evil demon do not have knowledge, but that is the correct conclusion (whereas Reliabilism about justification has the incorrect conclusion that those victims do not have justified beliefs).

Depending on what we think about the generality problem, it is possible that some of the Gettier cases are also counterexamples to Reliabilism about knowledge. Let us, for instance, take **Ginet's barns**. The process that generates the belief that there is a (real) barn at the side of the road seems to be reliable: after all, it belongs to the process type of forming beliefs about medium-sized objects under good lighting conditions, etc. Therefore, Reliabilism about knowledge would classify it as a case of knowledge, going against the verdict of at least some philosophers.

A different way of replacing the justification condition is given by the causal theory of knowledge:

CAUSAL THEORY OF KNOWLEDGE:

S knows that p if and only if:

1. S believes that p;
2. p is true;
3. S's belief that p is caused by the fact that p.

Note that the third condition of the causal theory of knowledge makes the first two redundant, and so the theory could be formulated more succinctly with just that condition (analogously, the third condition of the reliabilist theory of knowledge makes the belief condition redundant).

As a solution to the Gettier problem, the causal theory of knowledge seems to fail in a clear way. If we agree with the verdict that the subject in **Ginet's barns** does not know, then that is a clear counterexample to the causal theory, for the subject's belief is clearly caused by the fact that there is a barn by the side of the road. Moreover, the theory is also problematic regarding our moral and mathematical knowledge, for it is hard to explain how the mathematical or moral facts can enter into causal relations with our beliefs (although it is not, of course, impossible to generate explanations, appealing for instance to contingent psychological connections of the believer to the necessary facts).

As this brief survey of attempts to replace the justification condition as a way of dealing with the Gettier problem suggests, this strategy has not fared any better than the search for a fourth condition. This gives rise to what has been called "the Gettier problem problem," to which we now turn.

THE GETTIER PROBLEM PROBLEM

The Gettier problem consists in finding a characterisation of propositional knowledge without counterexamples. As our brief tour through different attempts at solving the problem suggests, there is no consensus among philosophers about the solution to the Gettier problem. The Gettier problem problem, then, consists of the following question: why have we not been able to solve the Gettier problem? The Gettier problem is a typical philosophical problem, which we can encapsulate in the question "What is knowledge?" The Gettier problem problem is *meta*philosophical: why have we not been able to solve this particular philosophical problem? By the way, an interesting characterisation of philosophy is that it is the only discipline that absorbs all of its meta-questions: the Gettier problem problem is itself, of course, a philosophical problem.

Something interesting happens in philosophy: many of its practitioners, including some of the historically most prominent ones, hold that philosophical problems are pseudo-problems. Indeed, that may also be an interesting characterisation of the discipline: the only one where that happens (try to find, say, a physicist who holds that the main issues in contemporary physics are pseudo-problems). That idea has been applied to the Gettier problem problem, with some philosophers suggesting that we have not been able to solve it because it is a pseudo-problem. In this section, we will examine two approaches of that sort. The first one derives from the American philosopher Willard Van Orman Quine, and the second from the contemporary British philosopher Timothy Williamson.

QUINE ON PHILOSOPHICAL ANALYSIS

To understand Quine's criticism, it is necessary to present the distinction between analytic and synthetic propositions, and the attendant distinctions between *a priori* and *a posteriori* and necessary and contingent propositions. As we shall see, Quine criticised the meaningfulness of all of those distinctions, but we shall first present them such as Quine inherited them from the early analytic tradition.

That analytic tradition in turn inherited the analytic–synthetic and the a priori–a posteriori distinctions from the German philosopher Immanuel Kant. The Kantian definition of analyticity lost its usefulness because it is applicable only to propositions of the form "S is P" (Kant accepted the Aristotelian thesis according to which all propositions are ultimately of that form). Kant held that an analytic proposition is one where the predicate is "already contained" in the subject. Contemporaneously the distinction has been refor-mulated as follows:

> **Analytic proposition**: a proposition is analytic if and only if it is true solely in virtue of the meaning of the concepts that com-pose it. (Propositions that are false in virtue of the meaning of the terms that compose it are sometimes called "contradictions." In some other contexts, the term is reserved for propositions that are logically guaranteed to be false.)

Let us explain the idea with an example. Take the proposition *pedia-tricians are doctors*. That proposition is composed of the concepts of *pediatrician* and *doctor*, as well as the concept of *inclusion*: it says, roughly speaking, that the group of people who are pediatricians is included in the group of people who are doctors. The proposition seems to be analytic because being a doctor is part of the meaning of *pediatrician*—*pediatrician* just means a doctor who specialises in the care of children. Analytic propositions, the traditional thesis holds, give no information about extra-conceptual facts.

> **Synthetic proposition**: a proposition is synthetic if and only if it is not analytic.

Synthetic propositions are true or false, not only in virtue of what they mean but also in virtue of what the world is like and, in con-sequence, they do have factual content; *pediatricians are rich*, for instance, seems to be an example of a synthetic proposition, for being *rich* is not part of the meaning of *pediatrician*. Whenever a proposition is true, its truth can in general be explained in terms of two factors: what the proposition means, and what the world is like. In the case of synthetic propositions, both of these factors are in full play, whereas in the case of analytic propositions, what the world is like does not contribute to making them true.

"A priori" and "a posteriori" are Latin phrases whose literal translations are "before" and "after." "Before or after what?", you might well ask. The Kantian answer is experience. Thus, a priori knowledge is knowledge that comes before experience, whereas a posteriori knowledge is knowledge that comes after experience. But Kant did not have in mind a chronological sense of "before" and "after." Kant held that no knowledge can be acquired without experience; all knowledge, he said, starts with experience. "Before" and "after" are therefore to be understood not in a chronological sense, but in an epistemic sense: what Kant meant was that some of our propositional knowledge owes its justification to our experience, whereas some other does not, despite the fact that all knowledge originates in experience in a temporal sense.

A priori: a proposition is a priori if and only if it can be justified
   without relying on sense experience.
A posteriori: a proposition is a posteriori if and only if it must be
   justified by relying on sense experience.

Notice that according to those definitions for a proposition to count as a priori all that is needed is that it *could* be justified without appeal to experience, whereas for a proposition to count as a posteriori it *must* be justified by appeal to experience. In other words, it is possible for an a priori proposition to be justified by experience, as long as it can also be justified without appealing to experience, whereas to be a posteriori a proposition must admit of no justification independent of experience. For instance, whereas it is possible to become convinced that 7 + 5 = 12 by repeatedly joining groups of 7 and 5 things and counting them, that experience is not necessary to justify the belief that 7 + 5 = 12, and for that reason the proposition that 7 + 5 = 12 would count as analytic (Kant himself held that the truths of arithmetic as well as geometry were actually synthetic, but the opposing view is much more natural, and Kant's arguments to the contrary are some of the most complicated of his philosophy). On the other hand, it is not possible to be justified in believing that it is raining without resting on some sort of experience—it could be, for instance, the sensory experience you have when you directly see the rain, or the auditory experience you have when you hear it, or more indirect experiences such as reliance on the testimony of your friend. For that reason, the proposition that it is raining counts as a posteriori. A posteriori knowledge is also sometimes called empirical knowledge.

Another notable characteristic of the definition of an a priori proposition also has to do with the fact that it appeals to ways in which a proposition can be justified. We can restate that definition by saying that a proposition is a priori if and only if it is possible for it to be justified independently of sense experience. But then a question naturally arises: possible for whom? Some mathematicians are able to follow and understand Andrew Wiles' proof of Fermat's last theorem, but we (the authors of this book) cannot. (Fermat's last theorem is the proposition that no three positive integers a, b, and c satisfy the equation $a^n + b^n = c^n$, for exponents n greater than 2.) Is the proposition stating Fermat's last theorem a priori? Can it be justified independently of experience? Well, Andrew Wiles and some other mathematicians seem to be able to grasp an a priori justification of it, but we cannot. Should we therefore say that the proposition in question is a priori because *someone* can justify it independently of experience? Or should we instead say that it is a priori for those who are able to grasp that justification, and a posteriori for the rest of us? If we go with the first option (namely, that a proposition is a priori just in case it can be justified independently of experience by *someone*), do we restrict the set of relevant subjects to human beings, or do we include any possible intelligence? These questions raised by the definition of a priori are interesting, but we do not aim to answer them here because they will not affect the discussion to follow.

According to the philosophical tradition that Quine criticised, all analytic propositions are a priori. The justification for this position is easy to understand: if there are analytic propositions, they are true purely in virtue of the meaning of the concepts that compose them. Anyone who fully understands a proposition will have to grasp the meaning of the concepts that compose it (or so it seems). But anyone who grasps the meaning of the concepts that compose an analytic proposition is in a position to know that the proposition is true, because that meaning guarantees that it is true. Therefore, it seems to follow that anyone who fully understands an analytic proposition is in a position to know that it is true, and their justification will not rest on any experiences they have (although of course it may have been necessary for them to have had experiences in order to grasp the proposition to begin with, the Kantian point is that these experiences are not part of the justification for believing the proposition). What about the reverse? Are all synthetic propositions a posteriori? Or is there a realm of knowledge that is at the same time synthetic and a priori? Kant thought that there was indeed such a realm; one of the fundamental aspects of his thought is that there is synthetic a priori knowledge. Those who hold this thesis are sometimes called *rationalists* (for they grant reason the capacity to know about the world without the help of experience); those who reject it, *empiricists* (for they hold that experience is necessary to know about the world).

A third distinction, related to the previous two, is that between necessary and contingent propositions. Some true propositions are *necessarily* true, or, as it is also said, are necessary truths. This is sometimes explained in terms of "possible worlds":

> **Necessary truth**: a proposition is necessarily true if and only if it is true in all possible worlds.

Of course, in order to understand that definition of necessary truth, we need to first understand the notion of a possible world. There are different philosophical theories of what possible worlds are, but for our purpose it suffices to say that possible worlds are ways the world could have been, where the "could" in question is to be understood in terms of the absolute notion of possibility that we discussed before. Thus, if you think that it is a possibility in this sense that there be talking donkeys, then there is a possible world where there are talking donkeys. However, it does not seem to be a possibility even in the absolute sense that this apple is green all over and also red all over. If so, then there is no possible world where this apple is green all over and red all over. So, a necessary truth is a proposition that it is true of every way the world could have been. A necessary falsehood (sometimes also known as a contradiction) is a proposition that is true of no way the world could have been. Propositions that are true of some ways the world could have been but false of others are called "contingent" propositions. Notice that the negation of a necessarily true proposition will be necessarily false, the negation of a necessarily false proposition will be necessarily true, and the negation of a contingent proposition will also be a contingent proposition.

According to the same tradition that holds that all analytic propositions are a priori and all synthetic propositions a posteriori, all analytic propositions are also necessarily true, whereas all synthetic propositions are contingent. Thus, according to this tradition, the three distinctions line up perfectly: on one side, we have the analytic, necessarily true, a priori propositions, and on the other side, we have the synthetic, contingently true, a posteriori propositions.

These three distinctions, as well as the position that they line up in the way just described, was central to the self-conception that analytic philosophers of the beginning of the twentieth century had of their own practice—in fact, the name "analytic philosophy" comes from there, although it has come to refer more to a *style* of doing philosophy than to any doctrine all of whose practitioners accept. The idea is that the fundamental task of the philosopher is to propose analyses of philosophically interesting concepts, such as the concept of free action or the concept of knowledge. The result of a successful conceptual analysis would be an analytic proposition. Thus, the idea was that just as we have the (allegedly) analytic proposition *All pediatricians are doctors*, we have to find a similar proposition that allows us to complete the proposition schema *An action is free if and only if . . .*, or, closer to our present concern, *S knows that p if and only if . . .* Given that analytic propositions are knowable a priori, this conception of philosophy fits well with the traditional idea that philosophers can carry out their job "from the armchair": that is to say, without appealing to experience to justify their analyses.

> **Analytic conception of philosophy**: the task of the philosopher is to provide analyses of interesting philosophical concepts, and the result of a successful analysis is an analytic proposition.

Quine's objection to the distinction between analytic and synthetic propositions can be summarised in the observation that the very notion of analytic truth depends on other notions, such as the notions of *meaning* or *synonymy*, that are just as obscure as it is. Moreover, the notion of meaning itself can only be explained, Quine held, by appealing to the idea of analytic propositions. We can explain what it is for two concepts to be synonymous (i.e., have the same meaning) by saying that certain propositions are analytic—for instance, we can explain what it is for the concepts *female fox* and *vixen* to be synonymous by saying that the proposition *something is a vixen if and only if it is a female fox* is analytic. But, according to Quine, we cannot break out of this small circle of interconnected notions, and so if we are skeptical about the intelligibility of all of them collectively (as Quine was) these circular definitions will be of no help.

Quine also had misgivings about the existence of a priori knowledge. He held that all beliefs are susceptible to be revised in light of experience and, conversely, that no particular belief needs to be given up in light of any experience. Rather, all of a subject's beliefs form an interconnected web, and when an experience necessitates a change in the web, no particular change is thus mandated, but rather the subject has the choice of retaining any beliefs provided that he makes the necessary changes elsewhere in the web. Thus, suppose for instance that Donald believes that it is not raining outside. Donald then looks out of his window and for all the world it looks like it is raining. A normal subject will of course now abandon his previous belief and start believing that it is raining. But Donald is not normal. Therefore, instead of revising his belief that it is raining, he revises instead his belief that everything is normal outside his windows, and starts believing instead that a complicated and subtle setup has been put in place in order to produce fake rain. This example illustrates Quine's point that no belief is immune to revision (Donald revises his belief that no complex and costly conspiracy is in place to make him falsely believe that it is raining) and also his point that no single belief *needs* to be revised in response to any experience (Donald does not revise his belief that it is not raining).

The example, however, concerns beliefs that are traditionally considered empirical. What about beliefs that are traditionally considered a priori, such as mathematical and logical beliefs? These too are not special, according to Quine, and are also susceptible to revision in light of "recalcitrant experiences," as Quine put it. As an example, Quine cited the strange experimental results in support of Quantum Mechanics and suggested that a change of logic might be one way of reacting to them. Interestingly, when other philosophers proposed precisely this—to reject classical logic in order to deal with quantum mechanical effects—Quine objected. But his objections were pragmatic and not epistemological in nature: he held that the loss of simplicity and familiarity involved in a change of logic did not outweigh the benefits in this particular case, but he did not give up the idea that even logic is in principle revisable.

But Quine's adventures in Quantum Logic bring up an interesting point. Let us go back to the rain example. That example illustrates how one deranged subject might react to an experience. We think, however, that Donald's reaction is unjustified. He should have just given up his belief that it is not raining instead of starting to believe silly conspiracy theories without evidence. The same goes, one might hold, for the cases of a priori knowledge that Quine considers. Faced with massive evidence that Mary does not love him, Joseph may react by giving up the law of no contradiction (which holds that it is not possible for both a proposition and its negation to be true) before he gives up his belief that Mary loves him. But this does not mean that the law of no contradiction is not a priori—it just means that Joseph is reacting irrationally, and so depriving himself of a piece of a priori knowledge readily available to him. What Quine says—that, faced with a recalcitrant experience, no proposition is immune to revision—is true *descriptively*, but not *normatively*: subjects may well react that way, but that does not mean that the reaction will be rational or justified.

Quine was as skeptical about this notion of normativity as he was about the notion of meaning, so his response to our objection is predictable: he thinks that the best a philosopher can do is describe how real subjects can and will react to experience, and that no sense is to be made of how they "should" react (outside of the practical considerations of overall simplicity and familiarity already alluded to).

As we see, Quine's rejection of the idea of analytic truths and a priori knowledge ultimately rests on pretty widespread skepticism about meaning and normativity in general. But, given this starting point, it is clear how Quine would have answered the Gettier problem problem had he bothered with it: he would have said that we cannot give a satisfactory analysis of the notion of knowledge because it is impossible to give satisfactory analyses of anything, and this is so because there are no analytic propositions. That is to say, Quine's response to the Gettier problem problem would have simply been a corollary of his rejection of the analytic conception of philosophy.

KNOWLEDGE-FIRST EPISTEMOLOGY

But general Quinean skepticism about analyticity is not the only way to solve the Gettier problem problem. A different position holds back from attacking the very idea of analyticity or conceptual analyses, but contends that there is no reason to expect that every interesting concept can be analyzed. On the contrary, it is to be expected that there be primitive concepts. According to some philosophers, most prominently Timothy Williamson, this is precisely what happens with knowledge. The solution to the Gettier problem problem, according to Williamson, is that we have not been able to find a satisfactory analysis of the concept of knowledge because it is a primitive concept. This Williamsonian position gives rise to a new way of approaching epistemology, knowledge-first epistemology. This program centers on the idea of inverting the traditional epistemological methodology. According to that methodology, exemplified in the attempts to solve the Gettier problem, we must find an analysis of the concept of knowledge in more primitive terms. According to knowledge-first epistemology, we must on the contrary take the concept of knowledge as a primitive and use it to clarify other epistemic notions.

One of the ways in which Williamson applies the program of knowledge-first epistemology is by defining evidence in terms of knowledge. Actually, what Williamson defines is the notion of the evidence possessed by a subject at a given time, which, according to him, is identical to the propositions known by the subject at that time:

Evidence is knowledge: the proposition p is part of S's evidence at t if and only if S knows that p at t.

As we shall see in the second part of this book, Williamson uses the thesis that evidence is knowledge to give an answer to skeptical arguments. But we are now interested in briefly analyzing the thesis in itself, independently of its use in answering skepticism.

What one calls "evidence" is a terminological decision, which means that it is important to avoid that the discussion about evidence devolve in a merely verbal disagreement. Williamson himself is aware of this danger, and for that reason he emphasises the functions that the notion of evidence must play. We shall do the same.

One of the functions of evidence (not discussed by Williamson) is, we think, that of delimiting the propositions that we must consider. If p is part of our evidence, then we should not even consider the possibility that p is false. Conversely, if we should consider the possibility that p is false, then p cannot be part of our evidence. Let us exemplify with a case: Jane knows that she left the car keys on the table. The proposition *the car keys are on the table* is part of Jane's evidence, and we can confirm this because Jane uses that proposition to delimit which possibilities she takes seriously and which ones she does not. For instance, Jane does not take seriously the possibility that the keys are in the bathtub.

So far, there is nothing here with which the defender of knowledge-first epistemology has to disagree, for we have said that Jane knows that the keys are on the table. But let us suppose that Jane does not know that proposition, because she is in a Gettier case with respect to it. Let us suppose, for instance, that her five-year-old found them and put them in the bathtub, but her spouse found them there and put them back on the table. We must suppose that the five-year-old does not do this habitually, for otherwise Jane would not even be justified in thinking that the keys are on the table—she should have considered the possibility that they were taken from there. But if that is indeed not something likely to happen at all, then Jane is in a Gettier case: she has a true justified belief in the proposition that the keys are on the table, but she does not know it. In that case, Williamson would say that the proposition is not part of Jane's evidence. But there is an argument against that assertion. That argument is based on two premises. The first one is that it is still rational for Jane to ignore possibilities incompatible with the proposition that the keys are on the table. Let us suppose, for instance, that Jane is thinking about what she needs to do before she leaves the house. Jane's plans in this regard would be perfectly rational if they assume that the keys are on the table. On the contrary, if Jane were to plan to spend half an hour looking for the keys, we would judge that plan as irrational. The second premise is the principle about the function of evidence with which we started this discussion: the thesis that a proposition p is part of a subject's evidence if and only if it is rational for that subject to dismiss possibilities incompatible with p. Given that it is rational for Jane to dismiss possibilities incompatible with the possibility that the keys are on the table even when she does not know that the keys are on the table, the principle about the function of evidence has as a consequence that not all of our evidence is knowledge.

The friend of the identity between evidence and knowledge can answer this argument in one of two ways: either by denying our thesis about the function of evidence or by disagreeing with us about which possibilities Jane can rationally dismiss. We leave as an exercise for the reader the evaluation of these two alternatives.

It is remarkable that our argument applies not only to propositions with respect to which we are in a Gettier case (that is to say, propositions in which we have a true justified belief but which we do not know) but also to justified beliefs in false propositions. For we can further modify Jane's case by supposing that the keys were left in the bathtub (unbeknownst to Jane). Even in this case, it is rational for Jane to make plans which dismiss possibilities incompatible with the proposition that the keys are on the table. If this is so, then not only are Gettier cases counterexamples to the thesis that our evidence just is our knowledge but so are (justified) false beliefs. In other words, if our argument is correct, then there is false evidence. This thesis can sound obviously false: after all, even if *what we take to be* evidence can be false, that evidence itself is false sounds like a contradiction. But let us remember that we are not interested in capturing all the details of the ordinary use of the word "evidence." On the contrary, what we are interested in, as we said before, is the epistemic function that the notion of evidence plays, and if we are right that one of its central functions is to delimit the range of possibilities that it is rational to consider, then it follows more or less immediately that the very idea of false evidence, far from being contradictory, is mandatory.

In the end, then, just as there is no clear answer to the Gettier problem, there is also no clear answer to the Gettier problem problem. One factor which we should not discard is the role that fashion and boredom play in philosophical discussions. It has not been fashionable for a while to work on the Gettier problem, in part because it has become a boring enterprise. That does not mean, however, that it is not pedagogically and theoretically interesting to return to this recent part of the history of analytic philosophy, and that is what we have tried to do in the preceding sections.

SUMMARY

In this chapter, we explained how the tripartite conception of propositional knowledge (explained in Chapter 2) must face the Gettier problem: the existence of cases of justified true belief that do not amount to knowledge. We explained Gettier's argument that there must be cases like that, as well as his recipe for generating them. We then examined two different possible reactions to the Gettier problem: adding a fourth condition to the tripartite conception to the effect that knowledge cannot be based on false belief, and replacing the justification condition altogether. We saw that both of those reactions must face serious obstacles. We then turned to an examination of the Gettier problem problem: why have we not been able to solve the Gettier problem? One answer to this problem derives from the Quinean dismissal of the very idea of analytic truths and a priori knowledge, and another from the recent development of knowledge-first epistemology.

FURTHER READING

Chisholm's sheep case appears in Roderick Chisholm, *Theory of Knowledge* (1989 3rd edition), Prentice Hall.

For the causal theory of knowledge, see again Alvin Goldman, "A Causal Theory of Knowing".

Ginet's fake barns case appears in Alvin Goldman, "A Causal Theory of Knowing", *Journal of Philosophy* 64 (1976), pp. 357–372.

Quine's attack on the notions of analyticity and a priority can be found in W. V. O. Quine, "Two Dogmas of Empiricism", *The Philosophical Review* 60 (1951), pp. 20–43.

Reliabilism about knowledge is proposed in the previously mentioned book by Armstrong: *Belief, Truth and Knowledge*.

The idea that there is a "double-luck" involved in Gettier cases can be found in Linda Zagzebski, "The Inescapability of Gettier Problems", *Philosophical Quarterly* 44 (1994), pp. 65–75.

The phrase "the Gettier problem problem" is from William Lycan, "On the Gettier Problem Problem", in Stephen Hetherington (ed.), *Epistemology Futures* (2006), Oxford University Press.

The project of knowledge-first epistemology is explained and developed in Timothy Williamson, *Knowledge and Its Limits* (2000), Oxford University Press.

The stopped clock example appears in Bertrand Russell, *Human Knowledge: Its Scope and Limits* (1948), Allen and Unwin.

The three-page paper introducing the Gettier problem is "Is Justified True Belief Knowledge?", *Analysis* 23 (1963), pp. 121–123.

Versions of the no false lemmas view are examined in D. M. Armstrong, *Belief, Truth and Knowledge* (1973), Cambridge University Press and Michael Clark, "Knowledge and Grounds: A Comment on Mr. Gettier's Paper", *Analysis* 24 (1963), pp. 46–48.

PART II
Skepticism

INTRODUCTION TO PART II

To a first approximation, it could be said that skepticism is a thesis regarding a subject and a proposition, and that it consists of the assertion that that subject does not know that that proposition is true. We all are, or should be, skeptical in this sense with respect to some subjects and some propositions. For instance, we should be skeptics with respect to any subject and the proposition that the number of stars in the Milky Way is even; that is to say, we should all hold that nobody knows that the number of stars in the Milky Way is even. But this is not a philosophically interesting kind of skepticism. It is not because to accept that kind of skepticism does not go against any of our initial attitudes. Recall the distinction we made in the Introduction to this book between easy cases, hard cases, and controversial cases. The easy cases are ones where our verdict about them comes easy. Do you know what you had for breakfast today? Do you know what is the 12,758th digit in the decimal expansion of pi? If you are anything like us, the answers to these questions are easy ("Yes" and "No," respectively). Then there are hard cases. Did anyone know that Biden was going to win the 2020 presidential election in the US? Or were those who believed it not justified enough to count as knowing it? We see room for reasonable disagreement regarding this question. It is a hard case. Then there are the controversial cases, by which we simply mean those cases on which there is significant disagreement. Some of those controversial cases will also be hard—that is to say, not only is there in fact disagreement but that disagreement is understandable from a rational point of view. Other controversial cases will be merely in fact controversial, even though they should not be. Sometimes, people attribute to themselves or others knowledge that they do not have, and sometimes they attribute lack of knowledge where knowledge is present.

Philosophical skeptics think that every case (in the area they are skeptic about) is easy, for we do not have knowledge in any of them. You do not count as a philosophical skeptic simply by holding that no one knows that the number of stars in the Milky Way is even, or even by holding that no one knew that Biden was going to win the election. Rather, to count as philosophical, your skepticism must concern cases where we would easily attribute knowledge. If, for instance, you hold that no one ever knows that it is raining, then you count as a philosophical skeptic.

We need to refine a bit more our general characterisation of philosophical skepticism, and to do it we can begin with nonphilosophical, common-sense skepticism. Why do we say that nobody knows that there are an even number of stars in the Milky Way? To answer that question, let us go back to the first part of this book. Let us suppose that we are in partial agreement with the tripartite conception of propositional knowledge, in the sense that we think that belief, truth, and justification are necessary conditions for propositional knowledge—although, let us also suppose, we agree with Gettier that they are not collectively sufficient. In that case, one can hold that subjects do not know a proposition either because it is not true, or because they do not believe it, or because they are not justified in believing it, or because they are in a Gettier situation with respect to it. Why do we say, then, that nobody knows that the number of stars in the Milky Way is even?

It is tempting to say that it is because the belief condition fails: we do not know of anyone who thinks that the number of stars in the Milky Way is even. But that is not the reason for our skepticism. Even if we found someone who does believe it, we would not ascribe knowledge to him or her. Our skepticism is also not due to the failure of the truth condition. Given that we apply to ourselves skepticism with respect to that proposition, for all we know it is true. And our skepticism is also not due to us thinking that we are in a Gettier situation with respect to that proposition. If that were the case, then we would have to believe that the proposition is true (for that is what happens in Gettier cases)—but we have already said that we do not believe that. Our skepticism is due to our thinking that the justification condition is not satisfied. We also think, however, that disbelief in that proposition is unjustified as well—that is to say, we do not think that anyone is justified in believing that the number of stars in the Milky Way is not even. Let us remember that in the first part of this book we distinguished three coarse-grained doxastic attitudes (or two, depending on whether we count disbelief as its own attitude or not): belief, disbelief, and suspension of judgment. Our skepticism with respect to the proposition that the number of stars in the Milky Way is even, then, is due to our thinking that neither belief nor disbelief in that proposition is justified. If we assume that, given any proposition and evidential situation, at least (and, probably, at most) one doxastic attitude is justified with respect to it, then our skepticism can be characterised by saying that only suspension of judgment is justified with respect to that proposition. And, indeed, this will be our more careful characterisation of skepticism: skepticism with respect to a set of propositions C is the assertion that the only coarse-grained doxastic attitude justified with respect to the members of C is suspension of judgment.

The difference between common-sense and philosophical skepticism, then, resides in the extension of C. Common-sense skepticism applies to a set of propositions with respect to which we would easily grant that we should suspend judgment, whereas philosophical skepticism applies to sets of propositions that we would normally suppose we are justified in believing (or disbelieving).

Now, some skeptical arguments target knowledge more so than justification. For instance, some philosophers have held that we do not know that we are not brains in a vat because our belief that we are not is not *sensitive* (in a sense that we will explain in Chapter 5), and they believe that sensitivity is a condition on knowledge (although not necessarily on justification). But even when a skeptical argument does not target justification directly, but rather knowledge, it will end up affecting justification as well. For let us suppose that a skeptical argument of that sort convinces us that we do not know that a certain proposition p is true. In that case, if the argument works then we know that its conclusion is true—that is to say, we know that we do not know that p. But then it is very plausible to suppose that we are not justified in believing that p either—the principle according to which if we know that we do not know that p then we are not justified in believing p may not be exceptionless, but it seems to hold in the general case.

There are three kinds of philosophical skepticism which are conceptually as well as historically important. In order of propositions affected, they are skepticism about induction, Cartesian skepticism and Pyrrhonian skepticism. Skepticism about induction derives from Hume's famous "problem of induction." Skepticism about induction is a possible solution (or dissolution) of the problem of induction, and consists in asserting that when the evidence in favor of a proposition is inductive—that is to say, when we are justified at best inferentially in believing that proposition, and when, in particular, the premises of such inference do not guarantee the truth of the conclusion—we are not justified in believing it. Assuming that we are not justified in disbelieving those conclusions either, the result is skepticism with respect to any proposition whose only possible justification is inductive.

Cartesian skepticism applies more widely: we are unjustified in believing not only those propositions whose only justification is inductive but also any proposition about the external world (given that the negation of an external world proposition is itself an external world proposition, we are not justified in disbelieving any of those propositions either, from where skepticism follows). Skepticism about induction does not affect those propositions about the external world that can be justified directly (non-inferentially). Cartesian skepticism does not affect propositions that are "internal" to the subject. For instance, according to Cartesian skepticism, I am only justified in suspending judgment with respect to the proposition that I have hands, but I am justified in believing that I have an experience as of having hands.

Pyrrhonian skepticism applies universally: it is a totally general kind of skepticism, according to which the only justified attitude with respect to any proposition whatsoever is suspension of judgment.

As we said at the beginning, philosophical skepticism is interesting because of the existence of arguments in its favor which cannot be easily dismissed. In what follows, we examine some of those arguments with respect to the three kinds of skepticism just distinguished.

INDUCTIVE SKEPTICISM

INTRODUCTION

Let us recall the distinction we introduced in the first part of this book between inferential and non-inferential justification. A belief is inferentially justified, we said, just in case its justification depends on the justification of other beliefs. More specifically, this has to be an *epistemic* dependence. Maybe the justification of every belief causally depends on the justification of other beliefs. Maybe, for instance, it is not possible to acquire an isolated belief. But when we say that the justification of a belief is inferential, we do not mean simply that it would not be justified unless other beliefs were also justified, but rather that *what justifies it* is, in part, the justification of those other beliefs.

Now, it is useful to model inferential justification in terms of arguments. When talking about arguments in connection with epistemology, there are at least two routes one can take. An argument can be defined relative to a person proposing it: an argument in this sense consists of a series of propositions, one of which (the conclusion) is claimed to be supported by the others (the premises). Claimed by who? By the person proposing the argument (who, by the way, can be wrong about the fact that the premises do support the conclusion). But there is a different characterisation of an argument, one which is more abstract and does not relativise it to a person. In this sense, an argument is simply a set of propositions, one of which (the conclusion) is supported by the others (the premises):

Argument: an argument is a set of propositions, one of which (the conclusion) is supported by the others (the premises).

DOI: 10.4324/9781003208440-7

There is a special kind of support that logicians, in particular, are interested in, and that is *deductive* support. The premises of an argument deductively support its conclusion just in case it is impossible for the premises to be true and the conclusion false. Using the terminology introduced in Chapter 3, the premises deductively support the conclusion just in case they logically entail it. If that happens, we will say that the argument is deductively valid (sometimes just "valid" for short):

Deductively valid argument: an argument is deductively valid if and only if its premises logically entail its conclusion—i.e., if and only if it is impossible for its premises to be true and its conclusion false.

We exemplify with what is perhaps the most famous deductive argument:

All men are mortal.
Socrates is a man.
Therefore,
Socrates is mortal.

But there are also cases where the premises support the conclusion even though they do not logically entail it (or, at least, that is the common-sense opinion that many have before encountering Hume's argument, which we will explain shortly). In that case, we say that the argument is *inductive*.

Inductive argument: an argument is inductive if and only if its premises support its conclusion but they do not entail it.

A difference between deductive and inductive arguments is that whereas deductive support is all-or-nothing (either it is or it is not impossible for all the premises to be true and the conclusion false), inductive support comes in degrees. Thus, one inductive argument may be stronger than another, in the sense that its premises offer its conclusion a greater degree of support.

What are examples of inductive arguments? A typical kind of inductive argument is sometimes called an argument by inductive enumeration, an example of which is the following:

ARGUMENT BY INDUCTIVE ENUMERATION

1. Piece of metal number 1 expanded when heated.
2. Piece of metal number 2 expanded when heated.
. . .

n. Piece of metal number n expanded when heated.
Therefore,
C. All metals expand when heated.

This kind of argument by inductive enumeration has a number of properties: its premises are particular (they refer to individual pieces of metal and their properties), whereas its conclusion is general, and its premises are about what happened in the past, whereas its conclusion includes also what will happen in the future. Some authors identify inductive arguments with arguments by inductive enumeration, and so conclude that inductive arguments "go from the particular to the general, and from the past to the future." But we do not think that it is a good terminological choice to make this identification between inductive arguments and arguments by inductive enumeration, and we think that the practice of defining an inductive argument simply as a nondeductive one (that is to say, as one where it is possible for the premises to be true and the conclusion false) is a better one. With our definition, then, there will be inductive arguments whose premises are not all particular, and also ones whose premises do not refer to the past. Here are some examples:

INDUCTIVE ARGUMENTS WHOSE CONCLUSIONS ARE NOT ABOUT THE FUTURE

1. Breads made from flour and water have been nourishing in all past instances.
Therefore,
C. This bread made from flour and water is nourishing.
1. This ticket is one of a billion in a fair lottery that was decided yesterday.
Therefore,
C. This ticket lost that lottery.
1. The newspaper says that this ticket has won the lottery.
Therefore,
C. This ticket has won the lottery.

Each one of those three arguments is inductive in our sense: it is possible for the premises to be true and their conclusions false. Notice also that in the first example the premise is general, and so that case is also an example of an inductive argument that does not "go from the particular to the general." It is worth pointing out here that sometimes arguments are "enthymematic"—that is to say, there are additional premises that are presupposed but not explicitly stated. In the newspaper argument, for instance, it is plausible to assume that there is one such presupposed (but not explicitly stated) premise about the reliability of the newspaper in question.

Indeed, we think there is probably no kind of proposition that could not be inductively justified. Think, for instance, about the fact that we can become justified in believing almost any proposition on the basis of testimony in its favor from a trustworthy but fallible source. This is inductive justification, for to say that the source is fallible is to say that it is possible for their testimony to be false (even if this is unlikely because the source is trustworthy). What matters in identifying whether an argument is inductive or deductive, then, is not the kind of premises or conclusion that the argument has, but simply whether it is possible for its premises to be true and its conclusion false.

We said that we may model inferential justification in terms of arguments, and we will soon explain what we meant by that. But we should note that some philosophers are wary of connecting logic and epistemology too closely. Logic, they think, has to do with abstract relationships between propositions, such as the relation of entailment, and there are no straightforward connections between those relations and epistemological properties of beliefs, such as being justified. While we sympathise with some of the arguments urging caution in the drawing of connections between logic and epistemology, we still think that it is useful to model inferential justification using arguments, as long as one is careful not to draw unwarranted consequences from those models (which is, in any way, a danger with any kind of modelling).

So, the idea is that the relationship between an inferentially justified belief and the beliefs on the basis of which it is justified is in important respects like the relationship between the conclusion and the premises of an argument. Thus, Jane may be justified in believing that Tarzan is in the cave because she is justified in believing that he is either in the cave or in the lake, and she is also justified in believing that he is not in the lake. In that case, we can model the structure of Jane's beliefs with the following argument:

DEDUCTIVE ARGUMENT MODELLING JANE'S JUSTIFICATION

1. Tarzan is either in the cave or he is in the lake.
2. Tarzan is not in the lake.
   Therefore,
C. Tarzan is in the cave.

Jane is justified in believing the conclusion of that argument because she is justified in believing its premises. Now, the argument in question is a deductive one (if you think about it, you will see that it is impossible for its premises to be true and its conclusion false). Does that mean that Jane's justification for believing its conclusion is deductive? We have to be careful here. The connection between Jane's belief in the premises and her belief in the conclusion is deductive, but the justification a subject has for believing the conclusion of an argument is not determined entirely by the deductive or inductive nature of the argument: his or her justification for believing its premises is also relevant. To a first approximation, one's inferential justification for believing a proposition is determined by two things: the strength of the inference, and one's justification for believing the propositions from which it is inferred (this is only a first approximation because there is a dispute, directly linked to the problem of induction, regarding whether what matters is the actual strength of the inference or what the subject is justified in believing about such strength). So, let us ask: what justifies Jane in believing the premises of the previous argument? Let us suppose that she is at the lake, and so she can just see that Tarzan is not there. There are interesting issues here about how perceptual justification works in cases like this, and we will canvass some of the options in Chapter 6, but most philosophers would say that perceptual justification is not infallible—Tarzan may have been well-hidden at the lake, for instance. So, Jane's justification for thinking that Tarzan is not at the lake is fallible (she is justified in believing it, but it could be false), and so her inferential justification for thinking that Tarzan is at the cave, which is based on that belief, will itself also be fallible. Moreover, we can suppose that her justification for believing that either Tarzan is at the lake or at the cave is based on the following inductive argument:

INDUCTIVE ARGUMENT MODELLING JANE'S JUSTIFICATION

1. In the past, Tarzan has always been either at the lake or at the cave at this time of day.
Therefore,
C. Today, Tarzan will be either at the lake or at the cave.

Inductive inferential justification always results in fallible justification, so Jane's justification for believing the first premise is also fallible, which gives an additional reason why her justification for believing that Tarzan is at the cave is itself fallible.

Let us conclude this section with another logical concept that will prove useful in our analysis of Hume's problem of induction: the notion of an *associated conditional*. To understand that notion, we first need to introduce the *material conditional*. Recall that, in Chapter 2, we discussed propositional connectives, and we listed some of them:

Some propositional connectives: not, and, or.

A material conditional is yet another propositional connective, but it can be defined in terms of the connectives we already know. We will write a material conditional as follows: $p \supset q$. "p" is the *antecedent* of the conditional, and "q" its *consequent*. "p" and "q" can be any propositions, atomic or molecular. What a material conditional says is that either its antecedent is false or its consequent is true—in other words, that it is not the case that the antecedent is true and the consequent false:

Material conditional: a material conditional, $p \supset q$, is true if and only if either p is false or q is true.

For instance, the material conditional *Joe is in Paris $\supset$ Joe is in France* is true, because either Joe is not in Paris or he is in France. On the other hand, the material conditional *Lucas is not studying ⊃ Lucas is sleeping* is false, because Lucas is playing video games (and so it is true that he is not studying but false that he is sleeping). Notice that nothing in the definition of a material conditional requires that there be any connection between the antecedent and the consequent for it to be true: the material conditional *Grass is green ⊃ Snow is white* is true because grass is green and snow is white, despite the fact that there are no connections (that we know of) between the greenness of grass and the whiteness of snow.

Now, the conditional associated with an argument is a material conditional whose antecedent is the conjunction of all the premises of an argument and whose consequent is its conclusion:

Associated conditional: the conditional associated with an argument whose premises are P_1, P_2, . . ., P_n, and whose conclusion is C is the material conditional *(P₁ and P₂ and . . . and Pₙ) ⊃ C.*

Why are associated conditionals interesting? One reason is that there is a tight connection between an argument's being deductive and its associated conditional: an argument is a deductive argument if and only if its associated conditional is necessarily true. If we go back to the argument that models Jane's justification for believing that Tarzan is at the cave, we can see that its associated conditional (*Tarzan is either at the lake or at the cave and he is not at the lake ⊃ Tarzan is at the cave*) is not only true but necessarily so: it is impossible for it to be false in the unrestricted sense of possibility that we are already familiar with. Thus, as we already know, the argument which models Jane's inferential justification for believing that Tarzan is at the cave is a deductive one (even though, as we also already know, that does not mean that Jane's justification for believing that Tarzan is at the cave is infallible).

But associated conditionals are interesting for an additional reason. We said that a subject's justification for believing the conclusion of an argument depends on two things: that subject's justification for believing the premises and the amount of support that the premises provide to the conclusion. But some philosophers think that what really matters is not the actual amount of support that the premises provide to the conclusion, but rather the amount of support that the subject is justified in thinking the premises provide to the conclusion—which will go hand-in-hand with the subject's justification for believing the associated conditional. As we said, the truth of a material conditional does not require any sort of connection between its antecedent and its consequent. But if the premises are true and the conclusion false—that is to say, if the associated material conditional is false—then the premises do not fully support the conclusion. And it is therefore very plausible to model a subject's belief in how much the premises support the conclusion by his or her belief in the associated material conditional.

Now, hopefully there will be a correlation between the truth of the associated conditional and the subject's justification for believing it—hopefully, that is, the subject will have a high degree of justification for believing true associated conditionals and a low degree of justification for believing false associated conditionals. But this need not always be the case. Go back to our example of the proof of Fermat's last theorem. We are in no position to understand any of it, but consider the situation of a competent mathematician who understands the proof, but is not sure that there are no mistakes whatsoever in it—that is to say, this mathematician is not sure whether the alleged proof is a real proof or not. In that case, and even assuming that the proof is a real proof, and therefore that its associated conditional is necessarily true, that does not mean that the mathematician in question can be certain of the truth of Fermat's last theorem on the basis of this proof alone. Rather, his justification for believing the associated conditional sets an upper limit to his justification for believing Fermat's last theorem.

Now, a more complicated question concerns what happens when the subject does not have any suspicions about the goodness of the argument in question. Does the subject need to be justified in believing that the associated conditional is true, or is it enough if he is not justified in believing that it is false? As we shall see, Hume's argument can be presented as relying on the idea that the subject must indeed be justified in believing the associated conditional, whereas some answers to Hume (notably, the inductive justification of induction) do not assume this.

THE PROBLEM OF INDUCTION

In Chapter 2, we introduced the idea that justification is defeasible—you can be justified in believing a proposition and then acquire more information which makes you no longer justified. In the previous section, we noted, in effect, that even deductive inferential justification is defeasible—both because your justification for believing the premises can be defeasible and because your justification for believing the associated conditional can be defeasible. Indeed, it is plausible to suppose that almost *all* justification is defeasible (after all, for almost any proposition you might believe, you would be unjustified in believing it if you are given sufficient testimony against it). We remarked on the defeasibility of deductive inferential justification to point out that it is not free of problems. But what we are interested in in this section is *inductive* inferential justification.

We also said in the previous section that we can have inductive justification for believing all sorts of propositions—not just generalisations or propositions about the future. We stand by that claim, but propositions about the future and generalisations play an important role both historically and systematically in the formulation of the problem of induction. We must make an important clarification regarding generalisations. By a generalisation, we mean a proposition like "All ravens are black" or "All metals expand when heated," which refer to an indefinite number of objects. These universal propositions are called "nomological" (from the Greek "nomos," meaning "law") or "lawlike" to distinguish them from "accidentally" universal propositions, such as "All the screws in Joe's car are rusted." Accidental generalisations can be thought of as conjunctions of a finite number of particular propositions. For instance, we can number all the screws in Joe's car and think of the accidental generalisation that all of them are rusted as the following conjunction: $screw_1$ is rusted and $screw_2$ is rusted and . . .. The distinction between accidental and lawlike generalisations is made because only the latter ones are considered to be good candidates for the rank of scientific laws: if a lawlike proposition is true, then it is a law, which does not happen with accidentally universal propositions. How is the acceptance of lawlike universal propositions justified? One answer consists in holding that such acceptance is justified by presenting those assertions as conclusions of inductive arguments whose premises are singular propositions that refer to observable facts.

The problem of induction is an argument whose conclusion is that we are never inductively justified in believing anything. The argument, which derives from Hume, starts from the idea that all inductive justification depends on the "principle of induction." The principle of induction can be given a general characterisation or particular formulations. According to the general characterisation, the principle of induction is an assertion that, added to any inductive reasoning, transforms it into a deductive one. The particular formulations are many: that the future will resemble the past (in the relevant respects), that the unobserved will resemble the observed (also in the relevant respects), etc. An initial problem is that the particular formulations of the problem of induction are not obvious cases of the general characterisation. For instance, it does not seem that a temporal formulation of the principle of induction can convert any inductive reasoning into a deductive one (because, as we already noticed, there are inductive arguments whose conclusion is not about the future). For our purposes, it will be useful to think of the principle of induction with respect to a given inductive argument simply as the associated conditional of that argument. Thus, suppose that we have an argument by inductive enumeration of the following form:

FORM OF AN ARGUMENT BY INDUCTIVE ENUMERATION

1. F_1 is G.
2. F_2 is G.
. . .
n. F_n is G.
Therefore,
C. All Fs are G.

The associated conditional for that argument will be the following: *(F_1 is G and F_2 is G and . . . and F_n is G) $\supset$ All Fs are G.* Notice that, indeed, adding that conditional as an additional premise to the argument would transform it into a deductive one.

Hume's argument starts with the claim that, in order to be justified in believing the conclusion of an inductive argument on the basis of its premises, a subject must be justified in believing the principle of induction. Given our decision to think of the principle of induction simply as the associated conditional, Hume's starting point amounts for us to the claim that in order to be justified in believing the conclusion of an inductive argument on the basis of its premises, a subject must be justified in believing its associated conditional.

Now, what kind of justification can we have for believing the associated conditional of an inductive argument? Could it be that those conditionals are necessarily true principles (maybe even analytic) whose justification is a priori? Let us remember that adding the associated conditional as a premise to an otherwise nondeductive argument transforms it into a deductive one. But if we examine the definition of a deductive argument—which says that its premises entail its conclusion, i.e., that it is impossible for its premises to be true and its conclusion false—we can see that the associated conditional of an inductive argument cannot be necessarily true. That is so because adding a necessarily true proposition as an additional premise cannot transform an otherwise nondeductive argument into a deductive one. For let us suppose that we have a nondeductive argument: that is to say, there is at least one possible world where all the premises of that argument are true but its conclusion is false. If we add a necessary truth to that argument, that possible world where all the premises are true but the conclusion is false will still exist—the premise we added will be true of that world because it is true of every possible world. Therefore, the associated conditional of an inductive argument cannot be a necessarily true proposition. Another way of seeing that this is true is to think about what would happen if the associated conditional of an inductive argument were necessarily true. The conditional says that it is not the case that the premises are true and the conclusion false. If the conditional were necessarily true, then that would mean that it is impossible for the premises to be true and the conclusion false. But the definition of an inductive argument goes precisely against this consequence: an inductive argument is one where it is possible for all the premises to be true and the conclusion false.

Could our justification for believing the associated conditional be a priori even if the conditional is contingent (that is to say, not necessarily true)? That cannot be accepted as a possibility by an empiricist. In fact, empiricism is sometimes defined as the thesis that all contingent truths are knowable only a posteriori. The idea is that if a proposition is contingent, then it is true of some possible worlds and false of others. To be justified in believing a contingent proposition, then, we must be justified in ruling out the possibility that we live in one of those worlds of which it is false. But how, the empiricist asks, can we discard that possibility a priori? After all, it is by definition possible that we live in one of those worlds, and if we do not appeal to any experience there does not seem to be any other kind of evidence that would allow us to eliminate that possibility.

The only alternative left open is that the conditionals associated to inductive arguments are justifiable only a posteriori. But on what empirical basis could we be justified in believing that if a sufficiently large number of objects that have some property F also have property G, then all objects that have F also have G? It seems that we cannot simply *see* (or otherwise directly experience) that conditionals like that are true. Therefore, if we are justified in believing them a posteriori, we are justified in believing them on the basis of an inference. Moreover, it seems implausible that the inference in question can be modelled by a deductive argument. Therefore, if we are to be justified in believing those conditionals a posteriori, it seems that we have to believe them on the basis of an inductive inference. An inductive argument by enumeration for this particular conditional, for instance, would look like this:

ARGUMENT FOR THE PRINCIPLE OF INDUCTION

1. In the past, when all Fs that were observed up to a certain time t were Gs, all Fs observed after t were also Gs.
   Therefore,
C. If all observed Fs are Gs, then all Fs are Gs.

But, of course, given that this is also an inductive argument, if this inference is to justify us in believing its conclusion, we would have to be justified in believing the associated conditional for this argument, namely: *When all Fs that were observed up to a certain time t were Gs, all Fs observed after t were also G ⊃ If all observed Fs are Gs, then all Fs are G.* That conditional, in turn, cannot be necessary (for reasons that we already explained), and so our justification for believing it can only be a posteriori. For the same reasons as before, it seems, moreover, that it can only be justifiably believed on the basis of an inductive inference. So it looks as if in order to be justified in believing the conclusion of an inductive argument we have to be justified in believing an infinite number of conditionals first. Or, if we follow Hume more closely and think that a single principle of induction would work for all inductive arguments, then we can only have inductive justification if we are justified in believing that this principle is true—but we can only be justified in believing that the principle is true on the basis of an inductive inference. So either there is an infinite regress of ever more complicated conditionals that we would need to justifiably believe in order to have justification even for the simplest proposition by an inductive inference, or there is a vicious circularity in the possibility of our justifiably believing that the principle of induction is true. In either case, it does not seem possible that we can have a posteriori justification for believing that the principle of induction or the conditionals associated to inductive arguments are true.

In summary, the argument in favor of inductive skepticism can be formulated thus (for ease of exposition, we formulate the argument in terms of the principle of induction, but an analogous one could be made for the associated conditionals of the relevant inductive arguments instead):

1. We have inductive justification only if we are independently justified in believing the principle of induction.
2. The principle of induction is not necessarily true.
3. The principle of induction is not contingent a priori.
4. The principle of induction cannot be justified empirically. Therefore,
5. We do not have inductive justification.

There are no interesting reactions to this argument that deny its second premise, but there have been reactions that reject premises 3 and 4, and others that offer non-epistemic justifications of induction. On the other hand, there have been philosophers who accept the conclusion of this argument, but who think that it does not represent a serious problem, for, according to them, we do not need inductive justification. In the remaining of this chapter, we will deal with some representatives of those reactions.

CAN THE PRINCIPLE OF INDUCTION BE JUSTIFIED A PRIORI?

The second premise of the argument in favor of inductive skepticism holds that the principle of induction is not necessarily true. Assuming that every analytic proposition is necessarily true, that premise has the consequence that the principle of induction is not analytic. It follows, then, that we cannot assume that the principle of induction can be justified in the same way in which analytic propositions are justified. And how are analytic propositions justified? A traditional idea is that analytic propositions can be justified a priori, through an analysis of the concepts that compose them. Thus, we can know a priori that a pediatrician is a doctor who specialises in children, and we can deduce from that analysis that a pediatrician is a doctor. Given that the principle of induction is not necessary, that route to its justification seems to be blocked.

But maybe the principle of induction can be justified a priori even if it is synthetic? Kant famously argued that there are propositions that are synthetic a priori. Kant did not distinguish in a careful way between a priori and necessary propositions, and so a Kantian answer to the argument for inductive skepticism can be presented either as a rejection of premise 2 or as a rejection of premise 3. In this section, we are interested in a rejection of premise 3 that has been put forward by Peter Strawson.

One way of presenting Strawson's position consists in calling attention to the difference between the principle of induction and the assertion that we are justified in believing the principle of induction. Let us consider a simple formulation of the principle of induction (the same idea can be applied to more complex formulations): that the future will resemble the past. The difference we are interested in, then, is that between these two principles:

PI: The future will resemble the past.
JPI: We are justified in believing that the future will resemble the past.

It is clear that **PI** is not analytic: it is not even necessarily true. But it is not obvious that **JPI** is not analytic. Strawson's position is, precisely, that **JPI** is analytic, true in virtue of the connections between the concepts of justification and the idea that nature is regular. According to Strawson, it is part of the concept of justification itself that inductive inferences can justify us in believing their conclusions (if they are good inductive inferences). For instance, it is a conceptual truth that, if we observe thousands of black ravens and no raven of any other color, then we are justified in believing that all ravens are black, even when we respect the obvious truth that it is not necessary that if all observed ravens are black then all ravens are black. Therefore, the conditional according to which if all observed ravens are black then we are justified in believing that all ravens are black is also a conceptual truth. And the same goes for the associated conditionals of every good inductive argument. Notice that the conceptual truth, according to Strawson, is that we are justified in believing those associated conditionals, not that those conditionals are true.

This adds an interesting wrinkle to the question of precisely what premise in the Humean argument is Strawson denying. If the Strawsonian answer consists in denying premise 3, then that would be because we do have a priori justification for believing in **PI**, despite the fact that it is synthetic, because **JPI** is analytic. The analyticity of **JPI** implies two things. First, if every analytic truth is knowable a priori and knowledge entails justification, then the fact that **JPI** is analytic entails that we have a priori justification for believing **JPI**. From this alone, it does not follow that we are justified in believing **PI**, however, let alone that we are a priori justified in believing **PI** (It would follow that we are justified in believing **PI**—although not necessarily a priori—if our beliefs about what we are justified in believing were infallible, but not many philosophers would accept this). Now, a second thing that follows if **JPI** is analytic is that **JPI** is true, and if **JPI** is true then we are indeed justified in believing **PI**—although not necessarily a priori. But if one agrees with Hume in that it is not possible to justify **PI** empirically, then it does follow from the analyticity of **JPI** that we are a priori justified in believing **PI**. Thus, it is not incorrect to say that the Strawsonian position claims that we are a priori justified in believing **PI**, but the route to that assertion is not direct.

At the core of this answer to the problem of induction lies Strawson's contention that it is a conceptual truth that we are justified in trusting induction. Philosophers impressed by Quine's rejection of the very idea of conceptual truths will, of course, not be moved by this. But one need not buy wholesale into Quine's philosophy in order to be worried about Strawson's strategy. If Strawson is right, then not only was Hume wrong in thinking that there was a problem with inductive justification, he was conceptually confused as well. If it is a conceptual truth that we are justified in trusting induction, then to ask whether induction can ever justify us (as Hume did) reflects a lack of grasp of the concepts involved.

To be fair to Strawson, this latter problem is connected to a larger issue with the conception of philosophy as providing analyses, an issue known as "the paradox of analysis." Suppose that one holds that the job of philosophy is to provide conceptual analyses of interesting philosophical concepts. The paradox of analysis is the problem that arises when we think about whether those analyses can be at the same time correct and informative. These two seem like good desiderata. The correctness constraint goes without saying. But so too does, it seems, the informativeness constraint: we are not sure what it takes for a belief to amount to knowledge, or for an action to be free, and that is why we turn to philosophers to tell us that. A good answer to our questions, then, would be an informative one: will give us what it takes to come to know what it is for an action to be free, or for a belief to amount to knowledge. But those two desiderata are in conflict: if an analysis is correct, then it is a conceptual truth, but if it is a conceptual truth, then anyone who grasps the concepts involved should already know that it is true. We can apply the paradox of analysis to Strawson's solution to the problem of induction: if Strawson is right that it is a conceptual truth that there is inductive justification, then anybody who already grasps the concepts of justification and induction should know this. But then the problem of induction should never have arisen in the first place.

There are different ways of replying to the paradox of analysis. One, of course, is to deny (perhaps with Quine) that the job of philosophy is to provide conceptual analyses. That will not help Strawson. Another one, inspired by Wittgenstein and some "ordinary language" philosophers, is to hold that conceptual analyses will indeed be trivial and non-informative, and that the requirement that they be informative is a mistake. According to this anti-philosophy conception of philosophy (not the only one, as we have already observed: philosophers seem to be particularly prone to professional suicide), philosophical problems are merely pseudo-problems which arise when ordinary language is somehow misunderstood by philosophers, and the real job of philosophy is to dispel those misunderstandings by showing them for what they are through a careful study of ordinary language. Someone who takes this line would say that Hume was indeed conceptually confused when putting forward the problem of induction. Yet a third possible solution to the paradox of analysis is to hold that an informative analysis makes explicit what is only implicitly contained in the concepts analyzed. Thus, it does not betray conceptual misunderstanding to think, for instance, that there is a problem of induction, but it does show that one has not yet made explicit for oneself everything that is implicitly contained in the concept of justification—for part of what is implicitly contained is that there is inductive justification.

The claim that we can know that **PI** is true a priori because **JPI** is analytic faces a version of the paradox of analysis, then. A defender of that claim can answer in one of the ways just briefly canvassed. But whatever such a defender says, the claim faces yet another problem. For suppose it is true that our concepts of justification and induction are such that it is analytic that there is inductive justification. Why would this have any normative consequences whatsoever? That is to say, even if we accept that according to *our* concept of justification the principle of induction is justified, we can conceive of alternative concepts, say the concept of *justification*★, according to which the issue of whether there is inductive justification★ is an open question. And the problem of induction can then be reformulated in the following way: why prefer our concept of justification to the concept of justification★? The answer which consists in saying that it is analytic that we are justified in preferring the concept of justification to the concept of justification★ does not seem very promising, for it is also analytic (or, perhaps, analytic★) that we are justified★ in preferring the concept of justification★ to the concept of justification. What is needed to go beyond this impasse is some reason for believing that our concept of justification is truer to the normative facts than the concept of justification★.

THE INDUCTIVE JUSTIFICATION OF INDUCTION

A notable property of good inductive arguments is that they work: for the most part, their conclusions turn out to be true. Some philosophers have attempted to mount an answer to the problem of induction on this basis. According to those philosophers, the principle of induction can be justified a posteriori, on the basis of its past success.

Hume's complaint against the a posteriori justification of the principle of induction is that such justification is condemned to be viciously circular. This is so because, according to Hume, the proposed justification can only be carried out through an inductive argument, and the principle of induction must be assumed true before it can be used to justify any inductive argument—including the inductive argument whose conclusion is the very principle of induction.

To see how proponents of the inductive justification of induction respond to this worry, let us pause to think which form, precisely, such justification would take. The idea is that the past success of induction would allow us to formulate an argument such as the following:

INDUCTIVE JUSTIFICATION OF INDUCTION

In the past, what was until then unobserved turned out to be relevantly similar to what had been observed.
Therefore,
The unobserved will continue to be relevantly similar to the observed.

Hume's circularity complaint can then be stated as follows: in order for that argument to justify us in believing its conclusion, we need to be justified in believing its associated conditional, namely, that if the unobserved turned out to be relevantly similar to the observed in the past, then it will continue to be relevantly similar in the future. But this associated conditional is itself a version of the principle of induction, and so in order to be justified in believing the principle of induction we need to be justified in believing the principle of induction to begin with.

Now, at this point, the defenders of the inductive justification of induction introduce an important distinction: the distinction between the principle of induction as a proposition (which, therefore, can be true or false) and the principle of induction as a rule of reasoning (which more or less reliably transmits truth from premises to conclusion, but cannot itself be true or false). This distinction is general. Consider, for instance, the valid logical rule that goes by the name of Modus Ponens. According to that rule, from a conditional and its antecedent we can infer its consequent. For example, if we know that if Joe is with his friends, then Joe is happy, and we also know that John is with his friends, we can infer that Joe is happy (we will see in the next chapter that justification need not always mirror logical relations in this way, but surely sometimes it does). When we reason in that way by Modus Ponens, we do not consider (at least not explicitly) the validity of Modus Ponens as an additional premise. Thus, what justifies us in believing that Joe is happy are our beliefs that Joe is with his friends and that if Joe is with his friends then he is happy. The validity of Modus Ponens is not part of our justification. Or, at least, what is not part of our justification is the proposition that Modus Ponens is valid. It is perfectly possible to be justified in believing that Joe is happy on the basis of the beliefs we mentioned without having any idea about the notion of validity, for example.

In the same way, we must distinguish, we were saying, the principle of induction as a proposition that may be true or false from the principle of induction as a rule of reasoning which may be good or bad. According to proponents of the inductive justification of induction, while it is true that we must presuppose (at least implicitly) that the rule corresponding to the principle of induction is a good rule when making any inductive argument, including the inductive argument for the truth of **PI**, we need not assume **PI** itself when making an inductive argument. Thus, we can inductively argue for the truth of **PI** by assuming, not **PI** itself, but the rule that it describes. The defenders of this solution to the problem of induction do not deny that it is circular in some sense, but they hold that the circularity in question is a kind of "rule circularity," and not "premise circularity," and they believe that, while premise circularity is always vicious, rule circularity need not be.

Who could be convinced by the inductive justification of induction? Let us suppose that someone tells us that they have discovered a new rule of reasoning. This rule, which we can call Modus Foolus, has the following form:

MODUS FOOLUS

If p, then q.
r.
Therefore, p.

Naturally, we are skeptical about the validity of Modus Foolus. But our friend tells us that he has an irrefutable argument in its favor:

If Modus Foolus is valid, then two plus two is four.
Seven plus five is twelve.
Therefore, Modus Foolus is valid.

This argument, our friend assures us, is solid: not only are its premises true but necessarily so (even setting aside the validity of Modus Foolus, a conditional with a necessarily true consequent is itself necessarily true). We could object that the validity of this argument in favor of Modus Foolus itself depends on Modus Foolus—if Modus Foolus is not valid, then our friend's argument is not valid either. But in reply to this objection our friend appeals to the distinction between premise and rule circularity. The argument, he holds, assumes only that Modus Foolus is a valid rule of reasoning, not the truth of the proposition *Modus Foolus is a valid rule of reasoning*, nor the truth of the associated conditional. Therefore, our friend continues, we can relax: given that Modus Foolus is valid, the argument just presented is a perfectly adequate justification of the proposition that Modus Foolus is valid.

Obviously, our friend is wrong and the argument in question does not give us any justification to believe that Modus Foolus is valid. Is there any difference between this case and the inductive justification of induction? An irrelevant difference is that Modus Foolus is presented as a *valid* rule of reasoning, that is to say, as a rule that cannot lead from true premises to a false conclusion. That is demonstrably false. For instance, from the true premises *If snow is black, then grass is green* and *The sky is blue* we can conclude by Modus Foolus the false proposition *Snow is black*. But this difference is irrelevant because we can concentrate on an alleged inductive rule. Let us consider, for example, the rule of counterinduction:

Counterinduction: If all the *X*s observed up until now have been *F*, conclude that the next *X* will not be *F*.

According to this rule, the fact that (for example) all the ravens observed up until now have been black justifies us in believing that not all ravens are black. Faced with the skeptic about counterinduction, it can be argued that, given that counterinduction has not worked in the past, that gives us reason to think that it will work in the future. Notice that neither the rule of induction nor the rule of counterinduction is presented as a valid rule, and so the aforementioned objection does not apply. But the counterinductive argument in favor of counterinduction is no more persuasive than the argument by Modus Foolus in favor of Modus Foolus.

Is there anything that distinguishes, then, the principle of induction, on the one hand, from Modus Foolus and the principle of counterinduction, on the other? Both Modus Foolus and counterinduction, considered as principles, are false, whereas (we believe) the principle of induction is true. But Hume's argument aimed precisely at raising doubts about our justification for believing the principle of induction. Can it be answered, then, assuming that it has failed? Maybe it can: several philosophers have held that it is not possible to rationally convince a skeptic, but that that does not mean that skepticism automatically wins. We will return to this point in our discussion of Pyrrhonian skepticism in the final chapter.

THE PRAGMATIC JUSTIFICATION OF INDUCTION

The two answers to the problem of induction that we have considered so far are direct responses, in the sense that they attack one of the premises of the Humean argument. Other answers are more concessive, for they accept the truth of the conclusion of that argument—there is no inductive justification—but try to explain why that conclusion is not as bad as it sounds. In this section and the next, we deal with two answers of this kind.

Let us start with a proposal from Hans Reichenbach. According to Reichenbach, even though Hume is right that there is no possible epistemic justification for our inductive practices, there is a kind of pragmatic justification (also called a "vindication" in the literature) of those practices. Reichenbach's basic idea is that if we take the choice between behaving inductively or not as a problem in decision theory, then there is an argument in favor of the conclusion that the only rational option is to behave inductively—that is to say, to act *as if* the principle of induction is true. This is compatible with holding that we are not justified in believing that the principle of induction is true, because sometimes it is rational for us to act as if a certain proposition is true even if we are not justified in believing that proposition.

To understand the details of Reichenbach's proposal, it is necessary to explain the fundamental concepts of the traditional decision theory which Reichenbach assumes. Let us begin with an example, and describe afterward the theory in question.

Let us suppose that Mary wants to meet with her friend, but she is not sure whether she is at the park or at the movies. To simplify the example, let us suppose that Mary has only two options: go to the park or go to the movies. The relevant possible states of the world are also only two: Mary's friend is at the park or at the movies. The possible results are four: Mary is with her friend at the park, Mary is with her friend at the movies, Mary is alone at the park, and Mary is alone at the movies. Let us suppose that Mary thinks that it is more likely that her friend is at the movies than at the park, let us say in proportion 70/30. Let us also assume that Mary has defined preferences over each possible result, and even that she can assign a number to each state (where a higher number represents a more preferred state). In particular, let us assume that Mary assigns 1 to being alone at the movies, 10 to being alone at the park, 30 to being with her friend at the park, and 50 to being with her friend at the movies (we will call these numbers the "utility" that Mary assigns to each state). With these assumptions in place, we can summarise the problem that Mary is facing with the following table:

	Friend at the park (30%)	Friend at the movies (70%)
Go to the movies	1	50
Go to the park	30	10

Going to the movies has two possible outcomes, one with a utility of 1 and another with a utility of 50, whereas going to the park also has two possible outcomes, one with a utility of 30 and the other with a utility of 10. Can we assign a unique number to the options, so that we can compare them with each other? Yes, and we can do it in several ways. Maybe the most direct way is to make a simple average, assigning 25.5 to the option of going to the movies and 20 to the option of going to the park. But the simple average only makes sense if Mary believes that it is equally likely for her friend to be at park than it is for her to be at the movies. It makes more sense, then, to take a weighted average, where the utility of each outcome is multiplied not by 0.5, but by the probability that Mary assigns to the corresponding state. Thus, the "expected utility" (another name for the weighted average we are talking about) of going to the movies is $(1 \times 0.3) + (50 \times 0.7) = 35.3$, whereas the expected utility of going to the park is $(30 \times 0.3) + (10 \times 0.7) = 16$. Going to the movies maximises expected utility, and is therefore the option that decision theory considers rational. In this case, the weighted average gave the same result as the straight average, but you can verify for yourself that this will not always be the case, depending on the utilities and probabilities that the subject assigns.

Let us now move from this example to its generalisation: decision theory. According to this theory, a decision problem is composed of a finite number of options, a finite number of possible states of the world, a utility function, and a degree of belief function. The basic idea, then, is that every decision problem can be understood in the following way: each option will deliver an outcome when combined with a possible state of the world; the utility function is a measure of how preferable that outcome is to the subject (compared with all the other possible outcomes); finally, the degree of belief function is a measure of how likely the subject thinks each possible state of the world is. Given these elements, and assuming that the utility and degree of belief functions satisfy certain formal requirements (for instance, this last one must be a probability function), the rational options will be the ones that maximise expected utility, where the expected utility of an option is an average of the utilities associated with all the possible outcomes of that option, weighted by the probability that the subject assigns to each outcome.

Let us note that the expected utility of an action is a function of the utilities of all its possible outcomes and the degrees of belief of the subject. There is a particular case where it is not necessary to calculate the expected utility of all the available options because it is possible to simply observe what the result will be: this happens when the utility of one of the options is always higher than that of any other option, regardless of which state of the world we are considering. Let us think, for example, of a variant of Mary's case: let us suppose that her utility function is as before except that she assigns 55 to being alone at the park. Independently of where her friend is, then, the possible consequences of going to the park are always preferable for Mary than the corresponding possible consequences of going to the movies. In that case, it is obvious that the utility calculation will deliver the result that going to the park maximises expected utility. When this happens, when there is an option A such that, for each possible state of the world, the utility of A in that state is greater than the utility of every other option, we say that A is a "strongly dominating" option, and in cases where there is a strongly dominating option, it alone will be the rational choice. Notice, moreover, that when there is a strongly dominating option, the degree of belief function is no longer relevant: whatever degrees of belief Mary assigns to the whereabouts of her friend, it is always better for her to go to the park. Strong dominance is not the only possible way this can happen: even if the utility that Mary assigns to being alone at the park is not greater, but rather the same as, being with her friend at the movies, it is still obvious that it is better for her to go to the park than to the movies no matter where her friend is. In general, when an option never has worse utility than any other one, and sometimes has a better utility than every other one, we say that this option is "weakly dominant," and weakly dominant options are also guaranteed to be rational.

(Caveat: this kind of dominance reasoning cannot be straightforwardly applied when the probability of the states depend on which action the subject performs. Thus, the lazy student makes a mistake when he reasons that not studying for the exam is the rational option, given that it is better to pass without having studied and also better to not pass without having studied. What the student is missing is that whether or not he passes is causally influenced by whether or not he studies. This complicates decision theory in ways that we need not address here.)

Going back to Reichenbach, his basic idea is that we have the option of behaving inductively and also the option of not doing it. To behave inductively is to behave as if we knew that the principle of induction is true, whereas to behave noninductively is to behave as if we did not know that. Thus, to open the faucet when we want a drink of water is to behave inductively, whereas to dance a polka in that same situation is to behave noninductively. As this example shows, whereas there will in general be one way of behaving inductively, there will be many ways of behaving noninductively, but this is not important for Reichenbach's argument. Our options, then, are to behave inductively or to behave noninductively. What are the relevant states of the world for this decision? The very principle of induction is what determines the answer to this question: the relevant states are those where the principle is true and those where it is false. We can summarise what we know so far about this decision problem in the following table:

	PI is true	**PI** is false
Behave inductively		
Behave noninductively		

Missing from this table are the utility and degrees of belief function. Beginning with utilities, Reichenbach argues in the following way. If the principle of induction is false, then the most likely outcome is that we will die no matter whether we behave inductively or not. This is so because if the principle of induction is false the only thing that is guaranteed is that the future will not resemble the past (or, more generally, that the unobserved will not resemble the observed), but we cannot know what specific form this non-resemblance will take. If we behave inductively in a world where the principle of induction is false, then we will soon die. But if we behave noninductively in that same world, then we will also soon die unless we are very lucky. This is related to the aforementioned fact that there are many different and incompatible ways of behaving noninductively. For instance, dancing a polka when we are thirsty is one way of behaving noninductively, but so is playing the piano. Given the indefinite number of ways in which the principle of induction can fail, Reichenbach argues, faring well by behaving noninductively in a world where the principle of induction fails is as little probable as faring well by behaving inductively in that world. Moreover, if one particular way of behaving noninductively did reliably result in favorable outcomes (for instance, if dancing a polka reliably resulted in our thirst being quenched), then we could figure that out inductively, and so the principle of induction would be true of that world after all (it is just that the world in question would have different regularities than the ones operative in the actual world). Therefore, the utilities corresponding to the outcomes where the principle of induction is false have to be the same (and low).

On the other hand, if the principle of induction is true, then behaving inductively will have an obvious advantage over behaving noninductively. If the principle of induction is true, then to open the faucet when we are thirsty will reliably result in our thirst being satiated, whereas dancing a polka (or behaving in any other noninductive way) when we are thirsty will reliably result in our death by dehydration. Thus, Reichenbach argues, if the principle of induction is true, we should assign a high utility to behaving inductively and a low utility to behaving noninductively, and so we can update the table in the following way:

	PI is true	**PI** is false
Behave inductively	High	Low
Behave noninductively	Low	Low

Notice, then, that what Reichenbach has argued is that behaving inductively is a weakly dominating option: things will never go worse for us if we behave inductively, and things will sometimes go better. Regardless, then, of our degree of belief in the principle of induction (and, in particular, even if we agree with Hume that we have no reason to believe that it is true), it is rational to behave *as if* it were true.

Something we pointed out at the beginning of this section, but which is worthwhile reiterating, is that the pragmatic vindication of induction is not a direct solution to the problem of induction: on the contrary, it starts from the assumption that the conclusion of the Humean argument against the possibility of inductive justification is true. According to Reichenbach, from an epistemic point of view, we are justified only in suspending judgment regarding the principle of induction, but from a practical point of view we are justified in behaving as if it were true.

POPPER'S APPROACH TO THE PROBLEM OF INDUCTION

Inductive arguments are invalid in the sense that it is possible for all their premises to be true but their conclusions false. Now, if inductive arguments have this "defect," why do we reason inductively? Why do we not rest content with deductive reasoning? Because only in inductive arguments do the conclusions say *more* than the premises—that is why they can be false even if the premises are all true. Deduction guarantees the transfer of truth from premises to conclusion, but does so at the price of not adding anything that was not already contained, at least implicitly, in the premises—it is limited to asserting explicitly some part of that content. As has been pointed out, the idea that in deductive arguments the conclusion is "contained" in the premises is not easy to clarify; it is probable that, in attempting the clarification, one ends up by repeating that deductive arguments cannot have all true premises but a false conclusion. Despite this difficulty, it must be true that inductive arguments have an "ampliative" character—otherwise, the problem of induction would not exist. Only inductive arguments are ampliative, and we need ampliative arguments, in daily life as much as in science. In summary, inductive arguments are invalid, but we are obligated to reason inductively. The conjunction of these two things gives rise to the problem of induction. Popper's approach to the problem of induction consists in claiming that we are not really obligated to reason inductively.

Popper was interested, in particular, in the question of the justification of lawlike generalisations. How are these generalisations justified? One answer consists in saying that the justification in question is gained by presenting the generalisations as conclusions of inductive arguments whose premises are singular propositions referring to observable facts, which thesis has, for obvious reasons, received the name of "naive inductivism." This inductivism clashes directly with Hume's argument. It must also face additional problems. According to this version of inductivism, it is possible to verify in a direct way, through observation, the observational propositions which are to figure as premises in inductive arguments. Such an observation would have to be prior to the acceptance (even if preliminary or tentative) of any theory, that is to say, it would have to be a kind of pure observation, free from any theory, something whose existence both psychologists and philosophers consider very dubious. Besides, naive inductivism holds that induction is not just the way we come to be justified in believing scientific theories but also the way in which we discover them—that is to say, it holds that science begins with observations and inductively discovers laws from them, which sounds highly implausible when it comes to laws regarding things that are not directly observable, such as atoms or intelligence.

In its sophisticated version, inductivism deals not with what happens in "the context of discovery," but rather only with what happens in "the context of justification," that is to say, it deals only with the issue of how to justify the acceptance of lawlike generalisations, without asking how such generalisations are discovered or invented. It also eschews the idea of pure observation which allows for the verification of observational propositions; it assumes that there is a set of observational propositions which are accepted (regardless of whether they are pure or theory-laden, and regardless of whether they have been verified or just confirmed) and which can serve as evidence in the evaluation of lawlike hypotheses. And lastly, this sophisticated inductivism does not pretend that the truth of those hypotheses can be proven, but rather that it is possible to assign them some probability or degree of confirmation on the basis of the available evidence. That is why this version of inductivism is sometimes called "probabilism" or "confirmationism." Confirmationism avoids some of the problems of naive inductivism, but must still answer the Humean skeptical argument.

The Popperian conception of science has as its starting point the wholesale rejection of inductivism in any of its variants. According to Popper, it is not possible to verify a lawlike generalisation, but it is not possible either to assign it any probability. It is possible, on the other hand, to refute it: a single counterexample is enough for that. No finite number of black ravens proves that all ravens are black, but one white raven proves that they are not. Due to this asymmetry between verifiability and refutability, Popper proposes this last one as a criterion of demarcation between science and "metaphysics"—to be empirical, a theory must be refutable. Against what one could naively think, irrefutability is not a merit but an inadmissible defect.

To test a theory empirically is, for Popper, to try to refute it—this is the only thing we can do to test theories, given that, according to him, it is not possible to verify them or even assign them any probability. If the theory is not refuted, then it is "corroborated" (a term Popper uses to emphasise that it is not inductive confirmation) and it can be provisionally accepted. Corroboration consists *only* in the failed attempt at refutation, and gives us no reason whatsoever to believe that the theory will continue working in the future. Popper must hold this, for any reason going from the past to the future which allows us to predict future success on the basis of past performance is an inductive reason.

But if in resulting corroborated, that is to say, in passing an empirical test designed to refute it, a theory does not gain any credibility regarding its possible future success, then why is a theory that is corroborated better than one that is not? Why, of two rival theories, is the one with the higher degree of corroboration the better one? Popper cannot give a satisfactory answer; for him, past success is not even a fallible indicator of future success. But then, that a theory is more corroborated does not indicate (not only does it not prove but it does not even fallibly suggest) that it is closer to the truth. In effect, the future failure of a corroborated theory can be even more pronounced than that of the less corroborated theory; in other words, the more corroborated theory may be refuted in the future, and its greater degree of corroboration gives us no reason to disbelieve this. Thus, Popper does not manage to establish a link between corroboration and verisimilitude (which means approximation to the truth, in Popper's terminology), that is to say, between what he takes to be the methodology of science and its aim.

Popper does not limit his rejection of inductivism to lawlike hypotheses but extends it as well to observational propositions which form the "empirical basis" of science—his "basic statements." This is a step that he is forced to take given that he holds (together with many, but not all, epistemologists) that to accept an assertion because it describes a fact that we are observing is to accept it for reasons that do not conclusively prove its truth. Popper's conventionalism with respect to basic statements is a consequence or part of his anti-inductivism. Indeed, in order to reject that perceptual experience, observation, plays a decisive role in the acceptance of observational propositions—to which it can only provide nonconclusive support, for they are propositions about physical objects, which exceed in content perceptual reports—Popper holds that basic statements are accepted as a result of a convention or accord among the members of the scientific community, a kind of conventionalism which severs the links between theory and experience.

SUMMARY

In this chapter, we have examined skepticism about induction: the thesis that inductive inferences do not justify. We started with some preliminaries: introducing the distinction between inductive and deductive arguments and the notion of an associated conditional, as well as the idea of modelling inferential justification with arguments. We then proceeded to present Hume's argument for skepticism about induction, at the heart of which lies the question of how we can be justified in believing the associated conditionals of inductive arguments (**PI**). We then presented two kinds of answers to Hume's argument: direct ones, which attempts to give a straight answer to Hume's question, and indirect ones, which agree with Hume regarding inductive skepticism but try to offer some kind of consolation. To the first class belong the ideas that we can be justified in believing **PI**. The a priori justification of induction, inspired by Strawson, holds that such a justification can be a priori, whereas the inductive justification of induction holds that it can be a posteriori. To the second class belong Reichenbach's vindication of induction and Popper's deductivism. Reichenbach holds that we can be practically justified in behaving as if **PI** were true, whereas Popper holds that we do not need to assume that **PI** is true either in science or in our daily lives.

FURTHER READING

A classic on the distinction between premises and rules is "What Achilles Said to the Tortoise", by Lewis Carroll, *Mind* (1895).

For a presentation and defense of the inductive justification of induction, see James Van Cleve, "Reliability, Justification, and the Problem of Induction", *Midwest Studies in Philosophy* 9(1) (1984), pp. 555–67.

For an analysis of Popper's position (in Spanish), see M. Comesaña, "Popper: experiencia y enunciados básicos", *Analisis Filosófico* (1991), and his "Racionalidad práctica e inducción: la propuesta neopopperiana de John Watkins", en Oscar Nudler (ed.), *La racionalidad: su poder y sus límites* (1996), Paidós.

Hume presents the problem of induction in his two main works: *A Treatise of Human Nature* (1739) and *An Enquire Concerning Human Understanding* (1748).

Popper's position can be found in his *The Logic of Scientific Discovery* (1959), Hutchinson.

Reichenbach's vindication of induction can be found in his *Experience and Prediction* (1938), University of Chicago Press.

Strawson's solution to the problem of induction can be found in his *Introduction to Logical Theory* (1952), Methuen.

CARTESIAN SKEPTICISM

INTRODUCTION

Skepticism about induction applies to a subset of our inferentially acquired beliefs: those that are the result of an inductive inference. It sets aside, therefore, non-inferentially justified beliefs (if there are any) and those that are justified on the basis of a deductive inference. For instance, one could hold that inductive skepticism applies to lawlike propositions, but not to those observational propositions which form the basis of the inductive inferences whose conclusions are lawlike propositions (although we saw in our discussion of Popper that many philosophers would hold that those very propositions are also inductively justified). Thus, the skeptic about induction holds that we have to suspend judgment regarding the proposition *all ravens are black*, but not necessarily regarding the proposition *the raven in the garden is black*. A least in principle, a skeptic about induction could concede that *some* propositions about the external world (that is to say, not about the mental state of the subject who believes those propositions) are justified.

Cartesian skepticism is an extension of inductive skepticism, for it holds that suspension of judgment is the only justified attitude not only with respect to every inductively acquired proposition but also with respect to any proposition about the external world. The definition of "external world" involved in Cartesian skepticism is subject-relative: a proposition is about S's internal world if and only if it is about some mental state of S, and it is about the external world (with respect to S) if and only if it is not about some mental state of S. Notice, then, that the mental states of some subject $S^\star$

DOI: 10.4324/9781003208440-8

different from S are part of the external world relative to S, but part of the internal world of $S^\star$. The idea of Cartesian skepticism is that it is possible to be certain about one's own mental states, but not regarding propositions about the external world. But it is worth making two clarifications at the beginning of our examination of Cartesian skepticism. First, Descartes himself was no Cartesian skeptic. The name comes from the fact that some of the arguments in favor of Cartesian skepticism have their origin in the *First Meditation*, although Descartes thinks he can answer those arguments in later meditations. But Cartesian skepticism has ancient roots—so much so that it is also known by the name "academic skepticism," referring to a phase in Plato's academy that lasted approximately between the third and the first century BC. Second, the idea just mentioned, that it is possible to be certain about one's own mental states (but not about the external world), is not an explicit part of the arguments in favor of Cartesian skepticism that we will examine (although it could be argued that it plays an implicit role in them).

THE MASTER ARGUMENT FOR CARTESIAN SKEPTICISM

To present the main argument in favor of Cartesian skepticism, we must talk about *skeptical scenarios* and *closure principles*.

> **Skeptical scenarios**: a *skeptical scenario* with respect to a proposition p and a subject S is a possible situation where a) S does not know that p, but b) S cannot distinguish that situation from a normal one.

Most people would think that in the normal situation we have knowledge, but the skeptic will of course disagree on this point. For that reason, the notion of a normal situation should be understood so as to be neutral regarding whether we normally have knowledge or not.

The subject's inability to distinguish a skeptical scenario from a normal situation is not to be counted as a deficiency on the part of the subject: rather, a normal, rational subject would not be able to make that distinction. For instance, the evil genius hypothesis from Descartes' First Meditation represents a global skeptical scenario—"global" because it applies to almost any proposition about the external world and to every subject. Thus, if Joe actually is the victim of a Cartesian evil demon, then a) he does not know that he has hands, and b) he cannot distinguish the situation he is in from one in which he does know that he has hands. Other skeptical scenarios include the possibility that we are brains in a vat connected to a supercomputer that generates experiences and memories indistinguishable from those of normal subjects as well as the scenario presented in the movie *The Matrix* (we already alluded to skeptical scenarios when discussing Reliabilism as a theory of justification).

We are also already familiar with closure principles from our discussion of Gettier cases. The principle we discussed in that connection was the following:

CLOSURE PRINCIPLE FOR JUSTIFICATION

If S is justified in believing p, and p implies q, and S deduces q from p and accepts q as a result of this deduction, then S is justified in believing q.

With the notion of a skeptical scenario and the closure principle defined, we are now in a position to present the master argument in favor of Cartesian skepticism that will occupy us for the rest of this chapter. Let us suppose that O is any ordinary proposition about the external world—for instance, the proposition that the subject in question has hands—and let us suppose that SS is any skeptical scenario with respect to that proposition and that subject. The argument is then the following:

MASTER ARGUMENT FOR CARTESIAN SKEPTICISM

1. If S is justified in believing O, then S is justified in believing *not-SS*.
2. S is not justified in believing *not-SS*.
   Therefore,
3. S is not justified in believing O.

In the remainder of this chapter, we will discuss this argument in detail, but it is worthwhile to make two preliminary clarifications.

First, we reiterate that the conclusion is general, in the sense that *O* can represent *any* proposition about the external world. Second, while it is clear what role skeptical scenarios are playing in this argument, the contribution of closure principles is more indirect. The first premise is not itself a closure principle, nor is it obviously a particular case of a closure principle. If we had defined a skeptical scenario as a possibility where *O* is false, then premise 1 would indeed be a particular case of closure principle. After all, if *O* is false in *SS*, then it is obvious that *O* implies *not-SS*, and the subject in question will then always be in position to infer *not-SS* from *O*. But it is not necessarily the case that *O* is false in every skeptical scenario. For instance, most of the propositions about the external world are true if we are dreaming right now—another skeptical scenario considered by Descartes in the First Meditation—or if we are in *The Matrix*.

How is premise 1 justified, then, if it is not always a particular case of a closure principle? Let us note that, even if *O* itself does not imply that we are not dreaming or inside *The Matrix*, the fact that we know *O* does imply that every skeptical scenario is false. Thus, even though not every skeptical scenario is incompatible with propositions about the external world, they are all incompatible with the subject's knowing those propositions. To get from this observation to premise 1 we need to make an additional assumption: that when subjects are justified in believing *O*, they are also justified in believing that they know *O*. This assumption may not hold in full generality. For instance, some people may think that they are justified in believing that their ticket in a very large lottery will not win, but they may be hesitant to claim that they know that it will not win. If they are justified in their hesitancy, then that situation may represent a counterexample to the assumption that when subjects are justified in believing *O* they are also justified in believing that they know *O*. But even though the assumption may not hold in full generality, it does apply in many cases—and, in particular, there is no reason to think that it does not apply to the cases at issue in the context of the argument for Cartesian skepticism.

Given that assumption, we can justify premise 1 as follows. First, we assume the antecedent of premise 1, that is to say, we assume that *S* is justified in believing *O*. From this and the additional assumption just mentioned, it follows that *S* is justified in believing that he knows *O*. But, as we explained, that *S* knows *O* implies *not-SS*. Therefore, from the assumption that *S* is justified in believing *O* it follows, by an application of the closure principle, that *S* is justified in believing that *not-SS*. We have thus derived the consequent of premise 1 from the assumption of its antecedent, and, therefore, we have proven premise 1 itself.

Partly because skeptical scenarios that do not imply that *O* is false complicate the discussion in the aforementioned way, and partly because skeptics are free to choose whatever skeptical scenario they like, in what follows we deal with skeptical scenarios that do imply that *O* is false.

THE CLOSURE PRINCIPLE

Let us examine, then, the first premise of the argument for Cartesian skepticism and the closure principle from which it can be derived.

In the first place, it is interesting that Gettier's formulation of the closure principle can answer several of the objections that have been made to simpler versions of the principle. Consider, for instance, the following:

> **Closure principle (naive version)**: If *S* is justified in believing that *p*, and *p* logically implies *q*, then *S* is justified in believing that *q*.

An objection to this naive version of the closure principle is that there can be logical implications that the subject is unaware of, in which case they would not be justified in believing the implied propositions. Notice that Gettier's formulation of the closure principle avoids this objection for it requires that the subject deduce *q* from *p* (which makes Gettier's version closer to what has been called a "transmission" principle, as we will soon explain).

But even careful formulations of closure principles such as Gettier's are open to criticism. In this section, we will examine three kinds of objections to closure principles: alleged counterexamples, allegedly untoward consequences, and alleged incompatibility with some other epistemological principles.

DRETSKE'S CASE OF THE DISGUISED MULES: CLOSURE VERSUS TRANSMISSION

Let us start, then, with alleged counterexamples. One of the most famous comes from Fred Dretske:

Dretske's mules

You are at the zoo, looking at the zebra exhibit. From where you are standing, you can see an animal that looks just like a zebra. Given that the situation is perfectly normal, you are justified in believing (and, indeed, know) that the animal in front of you is a zebra. That the animal is a zebra entails, of course, that it is not a mule cleverly disguised by the zoo authorities to look just like a zebra from where you are standing. Are you justified in believing that the animal is not just such a cleverly disguised mule?

Dretske thinks that you do not know, and are not justified in believing, that the animal is not a cleverly disguised mule, despite being justified in believing that it is a zebra. Is Dretske right?

To answer that question, let us look more closely at how the argument is supposed to work. Anne, let us suppose, is at the zoo, looking at a pen with an animal in it. The animal in question looks just like a zebra from where Anne is standing. Let us call the evidence that Anne acquires visually, E, let us call A the proposition *the animal in the pen is a zebra*, and B the proposition *the animal in the pen is a mule cleverly disguised to look just like a zebra*:

- E: the evidence Anne acquires visually
- A: the animal in the pen is a zebra
- B: the animal in the pen is a mule cleverly disguised to look just like a zebra

A obviously implies *not-B*, and we can stipulate that Anne is aware of this implication. What Dretske says is that E cannot justify Anne in believing *not-B*. And it seems that Dretske is right about this: after all, B is a possible explanation of E (that the animal is a mule cleverly disguised to look just like a zebra explains why it looks just like a zebra to Anne), and we cannot reject a proposition on the basis of some evidence which that very proposition explains. If we are careful with the stipulations regarding the details of the case, we can even make it so that B implies E: the disguise is so good that, at least from where Anne is standing, it is not possible to visually distinguish a mule so disguised from a zebra. In that case, if we rejected B on the basis of E, we would be rejecting a hypothesis on the basis of evidence which the hypothesis itself entails. As far as the evidence is concerned, things are just like B takes them to be—how could that evidence then be the basis for rejecting B? What Dretske's case shows is that it is perfectly possible for certain evidence to justify a proposition without justifying every other proposition implied by the first one. That the animal looks a certain way is a good reason to think that it is a zebra, and its being a zebra implies its not being a mule that has that same visual appearance, but that the animal has a certain visual appearance is not a good reason to think that it is not a mule with just that appearance.

Let us suppose, then, that we agree with Dretske as far as that goes. The principle that the case refutes is then the following:

Principle of justification transmission: If e justifies S in believing p and p implies q and S deduces q from p and accepts q as a result of that deduction, then e justifies S in believing q.

It is called a transmission principle because the idea is that the evidence which justifies p (namely, E) is transmitted through the inference and also justifies q.

It is easy to see that Dretske's case is a counterexample to that principle (if we agree with Dretske on his verdict about that case): let e be E, let us replace p by A and let us replace q by not-B. Our formulation of the closure principle (following Gettier) is pretty close to that transmission principle, but an important difference is that the closure principle makes no reference to E. In other words, while the closure principle does have the consequence that Anne must be justified in believing not-B, it does not say anything about what Anne's justification should consist of. It is true, on the other hand, that our formulation of the closure principle appeals to the fact that S deduces q from p and accepts q on the basis of this deduction. It could be assumed, then, that despite not explicitly mentioning the evidence which justifies p, the principle is nevertheless implicitly committed with the transmission of such evidence to q. For if S bases his belief that q on the fact that he deduced it from p, then it is plausible to suppose that q will be justified for S only if the reasons to believe p are also reasons to believe q. It could be naively assumed that this is always so: how could we have reasons to believe a proposition which are not also reasons to believe everything implied by that proposition? But Dretske's case seems to show that the question is not at all rhetorical, and that the situation it assumes impossible can easily happen. Maybe, then, as we said before, Gettier's closure principle is closer to a transmission principle, and so it is therefore subject to Dretske's objection.

But it is possible to formulate a closure principle that is not even implicitly a transmission principle:

> **(Alternative) closure principle**: If S is justified in believing p, and p implies q (and S knows this), then S is justified in believing q.

This more careful formulation of the closure principle does not assume that S's belief in q is based on his belief in p, although it does assume that S knows that p implies q. How is this possible? That is to say, how is it possible for someone to know that p implies q, and also know that p, without basing his belief that q on p? It is in fact not difficult to see how that can happen. For instance, any proposition implies any logical truth, but we do not believe that either it is raining or it is not (which is a logical truth) on the basis that grass is green.

Going back to the argument for Cartesian skepticism, this alternative closure principle is all the skeptic needs to justify the first premise of that argument: regardless of whether we deduce that (say) we are not brains in a vat from the proposition that (say) we have hands, we can easily realise that the fact that we have hands implies that we are not brains in a vat, and then an application of the alternative closure principle gives us the first premise. It is important to know, then, whether Dretske's case is a counterexample to this alternative principle. What the alternative principle implies is that Anne is justified in believing that the animal in the pen is not a mule cleverly disguised to look just like a zebra from where Anne is standing, but it is silent on what could justify Anne in believing this. Therefore, given that Dretske's argument is based on the observation that the appearance of the animal is not a good reason to believe that it is not a cleverly disguised mule, that case does not directly refute the alternative closure principle.

But one could think that it does indirectly refute it. For we must now face the following question: if it is not the animal's appearance that justifies Anne in believing that it is not a cleverly disguised mule, then what justifies Anne in that belief? Dretske seems to assume that when p implies q (but not vice versa?) the only thing that can justify us in believing q is our justification for believing p. We already said that that is not generally true, and we gave the example of arbitrary logical truths (which are implied by every proposition, but which we are not justified in believing on the basis of any arbitrary proposition). But if Dretske is wrong in thinking that that is the only way in which we can be justified in believing q, what other ways are there?

Some philosophers have suggested that when p implies q it can be p itself that justifies us in believing q, not the reasons we have for believing p. We will return to this suggestion in the next section, but for now it suffices to say that it is difficult to see in what sense p itself can justify q if what justifies us in believing p does not justify us in believing q.

For now, then, we have two possibilities: that our reasons for believing p justify us in believing q (a possibility which we must reject if we are going to defend the alternative closure principle), and that p itself, independently of our reasons for believing it, justifies us in believing q (a possibility that we shall reject for independent reasons). But there is a third alternative, and that is that we have reasons for believing that q which are independent of p. In Dretske's case, these reasons are not hard to find: in general, zoos do not cleverly disguise their animals in order to fool their clients, and, absent any special reasons to believe that this is what is happening in any particular case, it is perfectly reasonable to reject that possibility on the basis of those general reasons.

Once we see that it is possible to have independent reasons to believe that the animal in the pen is not a cleverly disguised mule, we must re-examine whether Dretske's case really represents a counterexample even to the transmission principle. For one may think that what justified Anne in believing that the animal is a zebra is not only the way it looks but also the fact that zoos do not in general disguise their animals. If this is the total evidence that justifies Anne in believing that the animal is a zebra, then that same evidence obviously also justifies her in believing that it is not a cleverly disguised mule. Our analysis of the alternative closure principle, then, reveals not only reasons for doubting that Dretske's case refutes it but also reasons for doubting that it refutes even the transmission principle. In any case, it is not obvious that Dretske's case is sufficient to raise serious doubts about the first premise of the argument for Cartesian skepticism. It is also worth noting here that the reliance on background evidence that pervades real cases of justified belief might give defenders of the no false lemmas view resources to reply to some of the counterexamples levelled against it.

CONSEQUENCES OF THE CLOSURE PRINCIPLE

Whatever we think about the alleged counterexamples to the closure principle, some authors have argued that we should reject it because it is incompatible with other very plausible principles. In this section, we will show that the closure principle is indeed incompatible with three other principles. However, after examining the conflict, it is not obvious that the only plausible way of reacting to it is by rejecting the closure principle—perhaps it is reasonable to reject one of the other principles instead.

Let us start by supposing, against the arguments examined in the previous chapter, that inductive justification is possible. Our first principle seems to embody exactly that assumption (although we will argue later in this section that it is possible to reject this principle and still admit the possibility of inductive justification):

Principle of Ampliative Justification: It is possible for a subject S to be justified in believing a proposition p on the basis of evidence e even if S does not have independent justification for believing some other proposition q such that e and q together entail p.

Consider, for instance, the following argument by inductive enumeration:

ARGUMENT BY INDUCTIVE ENUMERATION

1. Crow #1 is black.
2. Crow #2 is black.
3. . . .
   Therefore,
C. All crows are black.

What the Principle of Ampliative Justification says is that it may be possible for a subject to be justified in believing the conclusion of that argument on the basis of being justified in believing its premises, even if that subject is not also independently justified in believing some other proposition q such that adding q to the premises would transform the argument into a deductive one. This should remind you of our discussion of Hume's argument, which assumed that the subject must be justified in believing some such q. We will return to this point later.

Our two other principles are related to our discussion of Dretske's mules. There, we said that Dretske had a point when he insisted that Anne could not be justified in believing that the animal is not a cleverly disguised mule just on the basis of how the animal looks. The reason Dretske had for claiming this is that what we mean when we said that the mule is cleverly disguised is that it looks exactly like a zebra. Therefore, the fact that the animal looks like a zebra cannot be used as a basis for believing that it is not an animal that looks like a zebra (for instance, that it is not a cleverly disguised mule). And this idea seems to hold with full generality. If a proposition p perfectly explains another proposition q, then we cannot reject p on the basis of q. One way for a proposition to perfectly explain another is by entailing it. So, generalising and tightening Dretske's explanation for why Anne cannot reject the possibility that the animal is a cleverly disguised mule on the basis that it looks just like a zebra, we have the following principle:

Entailment: If p entails q, then no subject S can justifiably reject p on the basis of q.

But if we go along with this principle, and therefore we agree with Dretske that the fact that the animal looks like a zebra cannot justify Anne in believing that the animal is not a cleverly disguised mule, then we can ask: what, if anything, justified Anne in believing that the animal is not a cleverly disguised mule? Dretske, of course, argued that nothing does: that was the basis of his argument against closure. But we saw reasons for thinking that Dretske's argument is more successful against a transmission principle than against a closure principle. Nevertheless, the question remains a fair one: if we think (against Dretske) that Anne is justified in believing that the animal is not a cleverly disguised mule, on what basis is she so justified?

An answer that we briefly considered was that it was the fact itself that the animal is a zebra that justified Anne in believing that it was not a cleverly disguised mule. But how could p by itself, without any help from whatever justifies *it*, justify us in believing q? Coming back to our example: how can it be that Anne's belief that the animal is a zebra justifies her in believing that it is not a cleverly disguised mule if what justifies her in believing that it is a zebra (namely, the animal's visual appearance) does not justify her in believing that it is not a cleverly disguised mule? Our second principle assumes that this question does not have a satisfactory answer:

Mere Lemmas: If S is justified in believing p on the basis of evidence e, then p itself can justify S in believing some other proposition q (perhaps implied by p) only if e justifies S in believing q.

We call the principle "Mere Lemmas" because the idea is that if p is justified entirely by e, then p itself does not have justificatory powers of its own, independent of e—it is at best a mere lemma in the justification of other propositions (a "lemma" being an important step in a demonstration, but which follows from the starting points and is therefore eliminable without loss of validity).

Consider now the following four principles: Closure, the Principle of Ampliative Justification, Mere Lemmas, and Entailment. They are jointly incompatible: they cannot all be true. In the remainder of this section, we show how that incompatibility arises. The demonstration of the incompatibility gets a bit technical. If readers prefer to trust us that the principles are indeed incompatible, they can skip the following five paragraphs.

We will now show how those principles are incompatible. Let us suppose, following the Principle of Ampliative Justification, that S is justified in believing p on the basis of evidence e which does not imply p, without being independently justified in believing another proposition q such that the conjunction of e and q does entail p. Notice that p obviously entails the disjunction p or not-e. The closure principle, then, ensures that S is justified in believing p or not-e. But, of course, e together with p or not-e entails p (by the logical rule of "disjunctive syllogism"). Notice that p or not-e is equivalent to the material conditional $e \supset p$, which is the conditional associated to the argument which has e as its premise and p as its conclusion. Therefore, by closure, if S is justified in believing p on the basis of e, then there is a proposition which S is justified in believing (to wit, p or not-e) such that, together with e, entails p.

This comes close to being the negation of the Principle of Ampliative Justification, but it is not quite because that principle says that S cannot be *independently* justified in believing a proposition like that. Independently of what? Of his justification for believing p. Therefore, what we have said so far would not be a problem if what justifies S in believing p or not-e is not independent of p itself. There are two ways in which S's justification could be p-dependent: either p itself is part of that justification, or what justifies p is part of that justification. Given the Mere Lemmas principle, p itself can be part of that justification only if what justifies p (namely, e) is part of that justification. The only possibility left open, then, is that e justifies S in believing p or not-e. Let us note that e justifies S in believing p or not-e only if e justifies S in rejecting (disbelieving) the negation of that proposition—that is to say, only if e justifies S in disbelieving the proposition not-(p or not-e). But not-(p or not-e) (which, by one of the logical rules known as the "De Morgan" rules, is equivalent to e and not-p) entails e. Therefore, according to the Entailment principle, e cannot justify S in believing p or not-e.

There was a bit of logic-chopping in that last paragraph, so let us put the same point in a slightly different way. If e justifies you in believing p, then according to closure you are justified in believing $e \supset p$ (because that material conditional is entailed by p). That means that you are justified in disbelieving the negation of that material conditional. But the negation of that material conditional is just the conjunction e and not-p. Of course, that conjunction entails e, and therefore by the Entailment principle e cannot justify you in disbelieving it—which is the same as saying that e cannot justify you in believing the material conditional. But if e cannot justify you, then, by the Mere Lemmas principle, neither can p. Therefore, you have justification for believing $e \supset p$ which is independent of both e and p. But notice that $e \supset p$, together with e, entails p. So you have independent justification for believing a proposition ($e \supset p$) which, together with your initial evidence e, entails that p—and that is precisely the negation of the Principle of Ampliative Justification.

We will now exemplify the conflict between these three principles with a case. Let us assume that, in accordance with the Principle of Ampliative Justification, we are justified in believing that all ravens are black on the basis of our belief that all the ravens so far observed are black. Given that the proposition that all ravens are black entails that either all ravens are black or not all ravens so far observed are black, the closure principle entails that we are justified in believing this disjunctive proposition. If our justification for believing this disjunctive proposition were independent of our justification for believing that all ravens are black, then we would have a counterexample to the Principle of Ampliative Justification (for we would be independently justified in believing propositions which entail that all ravens are black).

We can evade this conflict between the closure principle and the Principle of Ampliative Justification if we hold that our justification for believing that either all ravens are black or not all ravens so far observed are black depends on our justification for believing that all ravens are black. Given that our justification for believing that all ravens are black depends on our justification for believing that all ravens so far observed are black, the Mere Lemmas principle entails that our belief that all ravens are black can justify us in believing the disjunctive proposition in question only if our belief that all ravens so far observed are black justifies us in believing that disjunctive proposition—that is to say, only if our belief that all ravens so far observed are black justifies us in disbelieving the negation of that disjunctive proposition. But the negation of that disjunctive proposition is (equivalent to) the proposition that all the ravens so far observed are black and not all ravens are black. That conjunction obviously entails that all ravens so far observed are black. Therefore, according to the Entailment principle, our belief that all ravens so far observed are black cannot justify us in disbelieving that all ravens

•

so far observed are black but not all ravens are black—that is to say, cannot justify us in believing that either all ravens are black or not all ravens so far observed are black. In summary, the closure principle requires us to be justified in believing the disjunctive proposition in question, whereas the Entailment and Mere Lemmas principle require that justification to be independent of our justification for believing that all ravens are black.

We have discovered an incompatibility, then, between the closure principle and the three other principles introduced in this section (the Principle of Ampliative Justification, the Mere Lemmas principle, and the Entailment principle). Several authors have concluded, on the basis of similar arguments, that we must reject the closure principle. Others, however, have argued that we should blame the Entailment principle instead. Some even reject the Mere Lemmas principle. In the remainder of this section, we will briefly develop a fourth possibility.

That fourth possibility obviously consists in rejecting the Principle of Ampliative Justification. This might sound crazy, particularly in the context of a book which takes for granted that inductive justification is possible. For, does not the rejection of the possibility of ampliative justification amount to the rejection of the possibility of inductive justification? The quick answer to that question is "No." In order to give the slightly longer answer, let us recall our reconstruction of Hume's argument to the effect that inductive arguments can justify us in believing their conclusions only if we are justified in believing the corresponding associated conditional. Hume himself believed that there was no possible justification for the associated conditionals, hence his skeptical position regarding induction, but we can agree with Hume regarding the necessity of being justified in believing the associated conditional without agreeing with him regarding the impossibility of such a justification. Thus, rejecting the possibility of ampliative justification is not equivalent to rejecting the possibility of inductive justification. For if we are justified in believing the associated conditional, and if our justification for believing the conclusion of an inductive argument depends on this justification, then so-called inductive arguments will not really be ampliative—adding the associated conditional as an additional premise turns inductive, ampliative arguments into deductive ones. Of course, it still behooves us to explain how it is possible for us to be justified in believing the associated condition-als of inductive arguments, and we have seen that that is not an easy task. But that it is not obvious how it is that we are justified in believing those associated conditionals does not mean that we are not, and we here adopt the position that we indeed are. In addi-tion, given that our justification for believing the initial premises of the inductive argument will itself be defeasible (if not literally inductive), the fact that we have now a deductive argument for a contingent conclusion does not mean that we have indefeasible justification for believing that conclusion. On the contrary, the defeasibility of our justification for believing the premises means that our justification for believing the conclusion is also defeasible.

It is undoubtedly true, then, that the closure principle is in con-flict with other plausible principles. But it is not at all obvious that the solution to that incompatibility consists in rejecting the clo-sure principle. We have not yet found, then, sufficient reasons for rejecting the first premise in the argument for Cartesian skepticism.

NOZICK'S THEORY OF KNOWLEDGE

A third reason to doubt the first premise of the argument in favor of Cartesian skepticism is its incompatibility with some theories of knowledge. This might seem strange, for the premise in question (and the argument more generally) does not concern knowledge but justification. But, as we said before, there are tight connections between the closure principle for justification and the closure prin-ciple for knowledge. Thus, if a theory of knowledge entails that we know that p but we cannot know that q despite the fact that p entails q, then we know that we do not know that q (at least, those of us familiar with the truth of the theory know this). And, in general, if we know that we do not know a proposition, then we are not even justified in believing that proposition. This is the flip side of the idea we appealed to earlier that if we are justified in believing a proposi-tion, then we are justified in believing that we know it (and the reader should keep in mind the caveats regarding the general applicability of that principle which we mentioned then). Therefore, theories which are incompatible with the closure of knowledge will also be in prin-ciple incompatible with the closure of justification—and, therefore, with the first premise of the argument for Cartesian skepticism.

One of those theories is Nozick's theory of knowledge, presented in his book *Philosophical Explanations*. To a first approximation, Nozick's theory is the following:

NOZICK'S THEORY OF KNOWLEDGE

S knows that p if and only if:

1. S believes that p;
2. p is true;
3. if p were false, S would not believe it;
4. if p were true, S would still believe it even if things were slightly different.

Nozick's theory is initially plausible. It can account, for instance, for the immediate perceptual knowledge of our environment. When we know that there is a table in the room because we are seeing it, for instance, Nozick's theory can explain this knowledge: we have a true belief that there is a table in the room; if there were no table in the room, we would not believe that there is one; and if there were a table in the room but things were slightly different, we would still believe that there is a table in the room. We said that the aforementioned is just a first approximation to Nozick's theory because the final theory incorporates elements designed to protect it from certain counterexamples. Given that we will not here deal with those counterexamples (although we will deal with others which cannot be avoided by those complications), it is sufficient for us to concern ourselves with the simple version of Nozick's theory.

Given certain assumptions, Nozick's theory is incompatible with the closure of knowledge. Do we know, according to Nozick's theory, ordinary propositions about the external world? It seems that we do. Let us take as our example the proposition that there is a table in this room. That belief is true, and so the first two conditions of Nozick's theory are satisfied. The third condition is also satisfied: if there were no table, we would not believe that there is one. And the fourth condition is also satisfied: if there were a table but the situation was slightly different—for instance, if the table were in a different part of the room—we would still believe that there is a table. Now, that there is a table in the room entails that we are not brains in a vat being stimulated to have an experience as of a table in the room when in reality there is none. But do we know, according to Nozick's theory, that this skeptical scenario is false? Let us suppose that it is, in fact, false, so as not to worry about the truth condition. We also believe that it is false, and therefore need not worry about the belief condition either. And the fourth condition does not seem problematic either: if the skeptical scenario were still false under slightly different conditions, we would still believe that it is false.

The problem arises with the third condition, sometimes called the "sensitivity" condition. Our belief that the skeptical scenario is false is not sensitive—that is to say, that third condition fails. This is so because, if the skeptical scenario were true, that is to say, if we were brains in a vat, we would still believe that we are not. After all, part of what makes the skeptical scenarios problematic is that, if we are in one of them, we have no way of knowing it. Thus, Nozick's theory has the consequence that we know that there is a table in the room, but we do not know that we are not brains in a vat in a table-less room.

Before analyzing this consequence of Nozick's theory, let us stop to examine in more detail how it arises. How can our belief that there is a table in the room be sensitive, if our belief that we are not brains in a vat in a table-less room is not? That is possible due to how we evaluate counterfactual propositions (or, more generally, how we evaluate subjunctive conditionals). A subjunctive conditional has the general form *If* p *were true, then* q *would be true*. When we assume that its antecedent is false, a subjunctive conditional is called a counterfactual conditional. How do we evaluate conditionals of that sort? We assume (perhaps contrary to what we know the facts to be) that the antecedent is true, we make the minimal modifications which that assumption forces us to make in order to maintain consistency, and we check to see whether the consequent is true in the resulting situation. Thus, let us suppose that we want to evaluate the conditional *If kangaroos had no tail, they would topple over*. We assume, first, that kangaroos have no tail. That assumptions force us to make other changes regarding what we believe about the world. For instance, if we assume that kangaroos have no tail, then we need to also change our opinion regarding what shape a kangaroo's shadow takes. But we do not make any gratuitous modifications. We do not assume, for instance, that the absence of tail entails the presence of longer arms. Given those minimal modifications necessitated by the assumption that kangaroos have no tail, do they topple over? Yes, they do. Therefore, we believe that the conditional is true: if kangaroos had no tail, they would topple over. On the other hand, we believe that the conditional *If July were less hot in Tucson, then it would snow in Tucson in July* is false. When we assume that it is less hot in Tucson in July, what we assume is that it is *a bit* less hot. To assume that it is so much less hot as for snowfall to be possible is to assume that things are gratuitously different from what they in fact are. Therefore, we take that conditional to be false.

Let us now go back to the failure of closure in Nozick's theory. That failure is due to the fact that our belief in the falsity of skeptical scenarios is not sensitive—whereas our beliefs in ordinary propositions are sensitive and also satisfy the other conditions. To say that our belief that there is a table in the room is sensitive is to say that, if there were no table in the room, we would not believe that there is one. Why do we take that conditional to be true? Because when we assume that there is no table in the room we assume, for example, that somebody took the only table in the room and placed it somewhere else. We do not make gratuitous assumptions, such as the assumption that, besides taking the table away, he also put a hologram of a table in its place. We therefore think that the conditional is true because we think that if there were no table in the room, we would be aware of its absence and we would not continue believing that there is one. To say that our belief in the falsity of the skeptical scenario is not sensitive is to say that, if it were true, we would continue believing that it is false. Why is that so? Because the very assumption that the skeptical scenario is true forces us to think that things are very strange—so strange that we cannot even know how strange they are. To assume that there is no table in the room does not amount to assuming that we are brains in a vat, but it is trivially true that to assume that we are brains in a vat amounts to assuming that we are brains in a vat. If there were no table that would be so for mundane reasons, and we would realise that there is no table. But if we were brains in a vat, things would be very strange indeed, and we could not realise how strange they are. That is why closure fails in Nozick's theory.

It is established, then, that Nozick's theory is incompatible with the principle of closure for knowledge. Does that give us sufficient reasons for doubting the first premise of the argument for Cartesian skepticism? Not obviously so. In the first place, we must face the aforementioned problem: the premise in question is about justification, not knowledge—although we said before that there are reasons to think that if closure fails for knowledge then it also fails for justification. But, in the second place, there are reasons to think that Nozick's theory fails, reasons which are largely independent of its treatment of skepticism. That is to say, regardless of what we think about the consequence of Nozick's theory according to which we do not know that skeptical scenarios are false, that theory has some other unacceptable consequences.

For instance, Nozick's theory seems incompatible with inductive knowledge. Let us see why. Let us suppose that we know that all ravens are black on the basis of the observation of a sufficient number of black ravens. Is our belief that all ravens are black sensitive? It would seem not. To see if that belief is sensitive, we must evaluate the following counterfactual: if it were not true that all ravens are black, then we would not believe that all ravens are black. And to evaluate that counterfactual we have to assume that not all ravens are black, make the necessary modifications, and see if we would then continue believing that all ravens are black or not. What is the minimal way of modifying reality in order to make it the case that not all ravens are black? Not by making it the case that some of the ravens that we have already observed are not black—that would suppose some kind of gratuitous mistake on our part, or something even more improbable. No: the minimal way of modifying things so as to make it the case that not all ravens are black would seem to be to make it the case that some of the not-yet-observed ravens are not black. If that were to happen, then we would continue believing that all ravens are black. Therefore, it would seem that our belief that all ravens are black is not sensitive and, therefore, it would seem that Nozick's theory is incompatible with the possibility of inductive knowledge. Of course, Nozick's theory is designed to have *some* skeptical consequences—to have the consequence that we do not know that skeptical scenarios are false. But the consequence that even inductive knowledge is impossible is unwanted, and sufficient, for many philosophers, to constitute a refutation of the theory.

In summary, we have seen that despite the fact that the first premise of the argument for Cartesian skepticism must face some serious objections, it would seem that it can overcome them. Let us then go on to consider the second premise of that argument.

DO WE KNOW THAT WE ARE NOT BRAINS IN A VAT?

According to the second premise of the argument for Cartesian skepticism, we are not justified in believing that we are not the victims of skeptical scenarios. What can be said about that premise?

SOSA'S SAFETY CONDITION

In the first place let us note that, as we said in the previous section, if sensitivity is a condition on propositional knowledge, then there is a good argument in favor of that second premise. For our belief that we are not brains in a vat is not sensitive: we would still believe that we are not even if we were. If sensitivity is a condition on propositional knowledge, then we do not know that we are not brains in a vat. Even more: we know that we do not know it (we can, for instance, reconstruct the argument just essayed). And, as we said several times already, it is arguably the case that if we know that we do not know p, then we are not even justified in believing p. Therefore, if sensitivity is a condition on propositional knowledge, then we are not justified in believing that we are not brains in a vat, just as the second premise says.

But we concluded in the previous section that it is not very plausible to suppose that sensitivity is, in fact, a condition on propositional knowledge. For instance, if it were, it would be difficult to see how inductive knowledge would be possible. But, admittedly, the idea that we do not know that we are not brains in a vat (and, more generally, the idea that we do not know that skeptical scenarios are false) is at least somewhat attractive. And even those of us who think that we should in the end reject that idea must explain why it is so attractive. Ernest Sosa has formulated a theory that promises to explain both things at once: why it is tempting to suppose that we do not know that we are not the victims of skeptical scenarios and why we actually do know it.

Sosa's theory is the following. There is a real condition on propositional knowledge which is very similar to the sensitivity condition, but which differs from it in important ways. Sosa calls that condition the "safety" condition. It is attractive to think that we do not know that we are not the victims of skeptical scenarios because that belief is not sensitive, and even though sensitivity itself is not a condition on propositional knowledge, safety is, and it is very easy to confuse sensitivity with safety. But our belief that skeptical scenarios are false is safe despite being insensitive. That explains why we do know, for instance, that we are not brains in a vat: we know it because our belief is safe, and it also satisfies all the other necessary conditions on propositional knowledge.

In what does Sosa's safety condition consist in, then? To present it we must first get into a somewhat technical issue in philosophy of language: subjunctive conditionals do not contrapose. To say that a conditional, *If A, B*, contraposes, is to say that it is logically equivalent to another conditional, *If not-B, not-A*. Some conditionals clearly satisfy contraposition. For instance, the material conditional of propositional logic is defined as the disjunction of the negation of its antecedent with its consequent—that is to say, a material conditional $A \supset B$ is defined as $\neg A \vee B$, where "$\supset$" stands for the material conditional, "$\neg$" for negation, and "$\vee$" for disjunction. $\neg B \supset \neg A$ is by definition equivalent, then, to $\neg \neg B \vee \neg A$, which is in turn equivalent to $\neg A \vee B$. Some argue that the indicative conditionals of natural languages have the same truth conditions of material conditionals. Be that as it may, it is plausible that at least some natural language conditionals do contrapose: for instance, when we say that *If John studies, then he will pass the exam*, it is natural to think that such a conditional is equivalent to saying *If John does not pass the exam, then he did not study*.

But there are philosophers who argue that some natural language conditionals do not contrapose, among them subjunctive conditionals. Let us suppose that Mary and Joe are invited to a party. Mary wants to avoid Joe, whereas Joe wants to hang out with Mary. Knowing that Joe will go to the party, Mary does not. In that situation this conditional is true: *If Mary had gone to the party, Joe would (still) have gone as well*; but its contrapositive (*If Joe had not gone to the party, Mary would not have gone either*) is false: the only thing stopping Mary from going to the party was that Joe was going to be there.

Why is it interesting, in the present context, that subjunctive conditionals do not contrapose? Because Sosa believes the following:

Sosa's safety condition

S knows that p only if, if S believed that p (perhaps in slightly different conditions), p would still be true.

It is easy to verify that Sosa's safety condition is the contraposition of Nozick's sensitivity condition. But, given that subjunctive conditionals do not contrapose, the two conditions are not equivalent. In particular, let us remember that our belief in the falsity of skeptical scenarios is not sensitive. However, that very belief is safe: if we believed that we are not brains in a vat, perhaps in conditions which are slightly different to the actual ones, it would still be true that we are not brains in a vat. To assume so radical a change as that we are brains in a vat amounts to considering a vastly different situation, not just some minor modifications.

Sosa's safety condition, then, is designed to explain two things: why it is tempting to think that we do not know that we are not brains in a vat and why, despite that temptation, we do know it. It is tempting to think that we do not know that we are not brains in a vat because safety is a necessary condition on propositional knowledge, sensitivity is the contrapositive of safety, and our belief that we are not brains in a vat is not sensitive. But that temptation is wrong because our belief is indeed safe (and also satisfies the other conditions for propositional knowledge).

Notice that when we say that our belief that we are not brains in a vat is safe we are assuming that we are indeed not brains in a vat. If we were, then of course our belief that we are not would not be safe (in addition to not being sensitive). Does that not amount to begging the question against the skeptic? That is to say, are we not assuming from the beginning that skepticism is false? If it were under discussion whether we in fact are brains in a vat, then to assume that we are not would indeed be question-begging. But what is under discussion is not whether we are brains in a vat, but whether we know that we are not. The Cartesian skeptic argues that we do not know it, but not on the basis of the premise that we are brains in a vat. That argument would be obviously valid, but equally obviously bad: the premise that we are in fact brains in a vat is even less acceptable than the assertion that we do not know that we are not.

But if it is indeed true that we cannot argue in a noncircular way that we are not brains in a vat, doesn't it follow that the Cartesian skeptic wins anyway? For, if we cannot argue noncircularly that we are not brains in a vat, doesn't it follow that we do not know that we are not brains in a vat? No: the fact that we cannot rationally convince someone who does not already accept a proposition that it is true does not mean that we ourselves do not know the proposition. Some philosophers are dialetheists: they think that there are true contradictions. As the best dialetheists have demonstrated, it is very difficult, perhaps even impossible, to argue in favor of the principle of no-contradiction without assuming it even implicitly. But very few conclude from this that dialetheism is true. Rather, it is supposed that some principles, such as the principle of no-contradiction, are so basic that it is not possible to argue for them noncircularly. Maybe that is what happens with the assertion that we are not brains in a vat (we will return to the question of what evidence we could possibly have for that proposition shortly).

Finally, note that when Nozick argues that we do know, for instance, that there is a table in the room, he is also assuming that we are not brains in a vat in a table-less room. If we were, then of course our belief that there is a table would not even be true, and therefore would not amount to knowledge.

Sosa may be justified, then, in asserting that our belief in the falsity of skeptical scenarios is safe despite being insensitive. But is Sosa right in thinking that safety is necessary for knowledge? Some have argued that it is not, on the basis of alleged counterexamples. Consider, for instance, the following case:

Halloween party: There is a Halloween party at Andy's house, and I am invited. Andy's house is very difficult to find, so he hires Judy to stand at a crossroad and direct people toward the house (Judy's job is to tell people that the party is at the house down the left road). Unbeknownst to me, Andy doesn't want Michael to go to the party, so he also tells Judy that if she sees Michael she should tell him the same thing she tells everybody else (that the party is at the house down the left road), but she should immediately phone Andy so that the party can be moved to Adam's house, which is down the right road. I seriously consider disguising myself as Michael, but at the last moment I do not. When I get to the crossroads, I ask Judy where the party is, and she tells me that it is down the left road.

The belief of the protagonist of that story that the party is down the left road is not safe because it could easily have happened that he had that belief while it was false, and that is so because he could have dressed up as Michael, and if that had happened then his belief would have been false. But, if we agree that the protagonist nevertheless knows that the party is down the left road, then this case represents a counterexample to safety as a necessary condition on knowledge.

It is not obvious, then, that Sosa's safety condition can explain why we know that we are brains in a vat despite our natural inclination to think that we do not.

ON THE ALLEGED SYMMETRY BETWEEN SKEPTICAL SCENARIOS AND NORMAL CONDITIONS

In the previous section, we analyzed a proposal from Sosa to explain how we know that we are not brains in a vat. But there is a very tempting argument in favor of the second premise of the argument for Cartesian skepticism. That argument starts from the idea that there is a symmetry between skeptical scenarios and normal conditions. One way of making that argument explicit is as follows. We all accept that, if the skeptical scenario were true, then we would not know that it is false (at the very least because of the truth condition on propositional knowledge). Given symmetry, we do not know that we are not brains in a vat even if we are not. Given that we can follow this argument, we know that we do not know that we are not brains in a vat. Therefore—appealing once again to the principle that if we know that we do not know that p, then we are not even justified in believing p—we are not even justified in believing that we are not brains in a vat—that is to say, premise 2 of the argument for Cartesian skepticism is true.

But we must now ask: what does that symmetry consist in, exactly? One possible explanation is to say that we have the same evidence in the skeptical scenario as we do in normal circumstances. How plausible we find this thesis will depend on our conception of evidence. According to a mentalist construal of Evidentialism, as we saw before, our evidence consists in our mental states. The symmetry of evidence between both cases, then, is true under a mentalist conception of evidence.

But some philosophers have denied that we have the same evidence in both cases. Let us recall, for example, that according to Williamson, the evidence a subject has consists of those propositions the subject knows. In the good case, we know several propositions that we do not know in skeptical scenarios. For instance, in the normal case, we know that we have hands, whereas in a skeptical scenario we do not. Given the closure principle, in the normal case, we know that we are not brains in a vat—but, of course, in the skeptical scenario where we are brains in a vat, we do not know that we are not. This Williamsonian conception of evidence, then, entails that there is an asymmetry between the normal case and skeptical scenarios. If Williamson is right, then the argument for premise 2 that relies on the evidential symmetry between those cases does not work.

Now, Williamson has to explain the *appearance* of symmetry: if the normal case and the skeptical scenarios are asymmetric, why are we so ready to accept that they are symmetric? In answer to this question, Williamson replies that the reason why skeptical scenarios strike us as symmetric to normal cases is that in skeptical scenarios we know so little that we do not even know what we do not know. If we were brains in a vat, we would not only continue to think that we are not but we would also think that we know that we are not. This is so because, if we were brains in a vat, our inner psychological life would be just as it is now, when we are not brains in a vat. Williamson's conception of evidence as knowledge denies that our evidence is determined by our internal psychological states, however, and so he denies that indistinguishability itself is symmetric. Subjects in the skeptical scenario cannot distinguish their situation from the normal one, in the sense that, for all they know (but not for all they believe), they are brains in a vat. But subjects in the normal case can perfectly well distinguish their situation from that of brains in a vat, for they know that they are not in that situation. In this respect, being a brain in a vat resembles being so drunk that one thinks that one is not drunk. When subjects are this drunk, they cannot distinguish their situation from being sober, but when they are sober, they can perfectly well distinguish their situation from being drunk.

But not everyone agrees with the Williamsonian conception of evidence as knowledge. It is important to note, then, that the alleged symmetry between the normal case and the skeptical scenario can be put into question even if we do not accept that conception. To begin with, we can explain why if we were brains in a vat we would not know it simply by appealing to the truth condition on propositional knowledge. Given a traditional conception of evidence, the justification condition is independent of the truth condition, and so the fact that in a skeptical scenario we do not know that we are not in a skeptical scenario does not imply anything about our justification for believing that we are not in a skeptical scenario when we are in a normal case. We can hold, then, that there are both symmetries and asymmetries between the normal case and skeptical scenarios. The symmetry can consist in the fact that, in both cases, we are justified in thinking that we are not in a skeptical scenario. A further, related symmetry, may be that in both cases we have the same evidence. All of this is still compatible with holding that there is an important asymmetry: in the skeptical case, we do not know that we are not in a skeptical case, whereas in the normal case we do. The argument for premise 2 based on the symmetry between normal cases and skeptical scenarios, then, does not appear to be sound.

WHAT JUSTIFIES US IN BELIEVING THAT WE ARE NOT BRAINS IN A VAT?

Even if we are right in rejecting the appeal to the symmetry between normal cases and skeptical scenarios, the Cartesian has still another reason in favor of the second premise of his argument. That second premise says that we are not justified in believing that we are not brains in a vat. Anti-skeptics reject this premise, that is to say, they believe that we are justified in believing that we are not brains in a vat. Faced with this assertion, the Cartesian skeptic can simply ask: what justifies us in believing that we are not brains in a vat?

One possible answer is that we are justified *a posteriori* in believing that we are not brains in a vat. Our evidence in favor of the proposition that we are not brains in a vat consists, according to this view, precisely in those ordinary propositions about the external world which the Cartesian skeptic denies we know. That we have hands, for instance, is our evidence in favor of our belief that we are not brains in a vat.

One problem with this answer arises from our discussion of Dretske's case of the disguised mules. There we said that Dretske is, in effect, conflating closure and transmission principles, and that, although his case may be a good counterexample to transmission principles, it is not obviously a counterexample to closure principles. That is so because one possibility which Dretske did not consider is that our justification to believe that the animal is a zebra depends on our (prior) justification for believing that zoo authorities will not disguise mules to look like zebras (and similar propositions). Thus, not every time that a proposition *p* entails a proposition *q* can we be justified in believing *q* on the basis of our justification for believing *p*—sometimes we can only be justified in believing *p* in the first place if we are already justified in believing *q*. And it is plausible that that is precisely what happens with ordinary propositions and the negations of skeptical scenarios. That we have hands entails that we are not brains in a vat, but our justification does not mirror that logical relation, but rather goes the other way around: we can only be justified in believing that we have hands if we have prior justification for believing that we are not brains in a vat.

One alternative consists in rejecting the presupposition of the question: nothing justifies us in believing that we are not brains in a vat, but this does not mean that we are not justified in believing that proposition, for we are justified in believing some propositions not on the basis of some evidence, but by default, so to speak. We will briefly re-examine this kind of position when we discuss Positism as an answer to the argument for Pyrrhonian skepticism.

Finally, a third answer to the question for our justification for believing that we are not brains in a vat consists in saying that we are justified *a priori* in that belief. Some philosophers have argued, for instance, that our justification to believe that we are not brains in a vat derives from the rationality of certain inferences. Consider, for example, the inference we engage in when we conclude that the picnic will be cancelled on the basis of the premise that it is raining. Even if it is not raining, we can still *assume* that it is and see what follows from that assumption. What follows (defeasibly) is that the picnic will be cancelled. Given that from the assumption that it is raining it follows (defeasibly) that the picnic will be cancelled, we have (defeasible) justification for believing the following conditional: if it rains, the picnic will be cancelled.

Now, it could be argued that something similar holds for the case of perceptual justification. Suppose that you are justified in believing that there is a red wall in front of you because you have an experience as of a red wall in front of you. Even when you do not have such an experience, you can assume that you do, and see what follows from that. What follows (defeasibly) is that there is a red wall in front of you. Given that from the assumption that you have an experience as of a red wall in front of you it follows (defeasibly) that there is a red wall in front of you, you have (defeasible) a priori justification for believing the following conditional: if you have an experience as of a red wall in front of you, then there is a red wall in front of you. Notice that this conditional is incompatible with you being a brain in a vat: if you were a brain in a vat, then it would be perfectly possible for you to have experiences as of red walls in front of you even when there are no walls (let alone red walls) in front of you. According to this line of reasoning, then, we are a priori (defeasibly) justified in believing conditionals that are incompatible with skeptical scenarios, and this is what justifies us in believing that we are not brains in a vat.

One problem which this response shares with other replies to the skeptic is that few people have reflected on the justification that, according to this response, they have at their disposal. But then, what justifies the vast majority of people who have never considered this answer in believing that they are not brains in a vat? One possible answer to this question is that the only thing that matters is that the justification be available, not that some subject in particular would have availed himself of it. But even if that is plausible for propositional justification, it is not for doxastic justification: the mental state of subjects who believe that they are not brains in a vat cannot be justified if the only justification available is one that they have never even considered.

So far, we have considered direct responses to the argument for Cartesian skepticism: responses which, in one way or another, reject one of the premises of that argument. A different kind of response is based on the difference between propositions and sentences which express propositions, and holds that there is a sense in which Cartesian skepticism is true, but another sense (at least equally important) in which it is false. We explore this contextualist answer to Cartesian skepticism in the following section.

CONTEXTUALISM

Bob is a fifteen-year-old who is five feet and eleven inches tall. "Bob is tall," says his grandfather. "Bob is not tall," says the basketball coach, explaining why he did not pick him as center. Despite appearances, the grandfather and the coach need not disagree. When the grandfather says that Bob is tall, he is expressing a proposition similar to the following: *Bob is tall for a fifteen-year-old*, whereas when the coach says that Bob is not tall, he is expressing a proposition similar to the following: *Bob is not tall enough to play center in the high school basketball team*. Both propositions are true and do not contradict each other.

A more explicit way of explaining this behavior of "tall" in English is by saying that the meaning of that word in any occasion of use is determined by two things: a component of meaning which is independent of the context in which the word is used, and the context in which it is used on each occasion. The meaning of "tall" can be vaguely specified as "sufficiently taller than the average X," where "X" is a reference class that is determined by context. Is it not circular to say that the character of "tall" is "sufficiently *taller* than the average X"? No: "taller than" is not context-dependent in the same way that "tall" is (although "sufficiently" might be context-dependent). Thus, when the grandfather says "Bob is tall," he expresses the proposition *Bob is sufficiently taller than the average fifteen-year-old*, whereas when the coach says "Bob is not tall," he is expressing the proposition *Bob is not sufficiently taller than the average center in the high-school basketball team*. Again, both propositions are true and do not contradict each other.

One version of epistemic contextualism is the thesis that "justified" behaves just like "tall" in the relevant ways—that is to say, that the meaning of "justified" (and its cognates) depends on its context of use in the same way in which the meaning of "tall" depends on the context of use. According to this thesis, the meaning of "justified" is more or less the following: *justified to degree X*, where "X" is a contextually determined amount of justification. Is it not circular to say that the character of "justified" is "*justified* to degree X"? No: "justified to degree X" is not context-dependent in the same way that "justified" is. The idea here is that the degree of justification that a belief has is not context-dependent, but that the degree of justification that a belief *must* have in order to count as justified *simpliciter* is context-dependent—in the same way that the height of a person is not context-dependent, but how high they must be in order to count as "tall" is context-dependent.

Armed with this conception of the meaning of "justified," the contextualist formulates the following analysis of the argument for Cartesian skepticism. Our beliefs in ordinary propositions and the negations of skeptical scenarios are justified to a moderate degree. That moderate degree of justification is sufficient for them to count as justified *simpliciter* in normal contexts, but not sufficient for them to count as justified *simpliciter* in skeptical contexts. Normal contexts are contexts that require only a moderate amount of justification for beliefs to count as justified *simpliciter*, whereas skeptical contexts are contexts that require a higher degree of justification for beliefs to count as justified *simpliciter*. Thus, when Jane says, in a normal context, "I am justified in believing that there is a table in the room," she expresses the proposition *My justification for believing that there is a table in the room is at least of a moderate degree*, whereas when the Cartesian skeptic says, "Jane is not justified in believing that there is a table in the room," he expresses the proposition *Jane's belief that there is a table in the room is not justified to a very high degree* (or something to that effect). These propositions may well both be true, and they do not contradict each other.

What determines whether a context is normal or skeptical? Many contextualists think that a decisive factor is the attention that participants in the conversation give to skeptical scenarios. If skeptical scenarios are not part of the discussion, then the context tends to be normal, whereas if skeptical scenarios are part of the discussion, then the context tends to be skeptical. In this sense, the skeptic has an advantage, for just mentioning skeptical scenarios will tend to turn the context into a skeptical one.

Let us examine in more detail the contextualist analysis of the argument for Cartesian skepticism. The contextualist will say that both the second premise and the conclusion of that argument have context-dependent expressions. Thus, if we are in a normal context, both the second premise and the conclusion of that argument will express false propositions, whereas if we are in a skeptical context, they will express true propositions. That is to say, if we are in a normal context the sentences "Sophie is not justified in believing that there is a table in the room" and "Sophie is not justified in believing that she is not a brain in a vat" will express false propositions, whereas if we are in a skeptical context those same sentences will express true propositions. Notice something important: if we are in a normal context, then the sentence "Sophie is justified in believing that she is not a brain in a vat" will express, as we said, a true proposition (namely, the proposition that Sophie's justification for believing that she is not a brain in a vat is high enough). But if we *say*, in that context, "Sophie is justified in believing that she is not a brain in a vat," we run the risk of changing the context to a skeptical one, for we have mentioned the possibility that Sophie is a brain in a vat.

What happens, according to contextualism, with the first premise of the argument for Cartesian skepticism? The standard contextualist answer is that, assuming that it is not possible to change context mid-sentence, this first premise will always be true. For if the context is such that it makes the antecedent of the conditional true (that is to say, if the level of justification required by the context is middling), then it also makes the consequent true. Notice that this take on the first premise of the skeptical argument relies on the idea that we have the same level of justification for believing that we are not brains in a vat as we do for believing ordinary propositions.

In summary, contextualism as a response to Cartesian skepticism is the combination of two theses: a linguistic one, according to which the meaning of "justified" varies with context, and an epistemic one, according to which we have a moderate amount of justification to believe both ordinary propositions as well as the negations of skeptical scenarios. Discussions of contextualism in the literature tend to focus on the first, linguistic thesis, but we think that the second thesis is at least as important as the first one. For what reasons does the contextualist have for saying, in particular, that we have a moderate degree of justification for believing that we are not brains in a vat? This is precisely what the Cartesian skeptic denies, and the contextualist *qua* contextualist has nothing to add to our discussion of that question. Contextualism, then, is incomplete as an answer to Cartesian skepticism, for it leaves open the question of what justifies us (even to a moderate degree) in believing that we are not brains in a vat.

SUMMARY

In this chapter, we have examined Cartesian skepticism, which is the thesis that we are not justified in believing any proposition about the external world. We began by explaining what we called the master argument for Cartesian skepticism, and we examined a number of replies to it. Given the relevance of closure principles to the first premise of the master argument, we examined a number of challenges to closure principles: Dretske's case of the disguised mules, the incompatibility of closure principles with other plausible epistemic principles, as well as its incompatibility with Nozick's theory of knowledge. None of those challenges proved fatal to closure principles. We turned next to the second premise of the master argument, according to which we are not justified in believing that we are not brains in a vat—and, more generally, we are not justified in believing that skeptical scenarios do not obtain. We examined Sosa's safety condition on knowledge as a potential explanation for why we are tempted to think that we do not know that we are not brains in a vat despite the fact that we do know it, as well as the symmetries and asymmetries there are between skeptical scenarios and normal situations (and the bearing of those symmetries and asymmetries regarding whether we know or are justified in believing that skeptical scenarios do not obtain). We then asked the question of *what* can justify us in believing that we are not brains in a vat, and we canvassed some answers to that question. Finally, we presented contextualism about "justification" as a way to offer a conciliatory position between skepticism and anti-skepticism, but we also indicated that contextualism by itself, as theory in the philosophy of language, does not seem capable of delivering on that promise, for it rests on the undefended assumption that we have a moderate amount of justification for believing that we are not brains in a vat.

FURTHER READING

Although Descartes was not a skeptic, one of the best introductions to Cartesian skepticism still is his *Meditations on First Philosophy*, originally published in 1641. For an English translation, see R. Descartes, *Meditations on First Philosophy* (M. Moriarty, Trans.) (2008), Oxford University Press.

Cohen defends the view that we have *a priori* justification for believing that we are not brains in a vat in his "Bootstrapping, Defeasible Reasoning and *a priori* Justification", *Philosophical Perspectives* 24 (2010), pp. 141–159.

For a debate regarding the closure principle, see the exchange between John Hawthorne and Fred Dretske, *Contemporary Debates in Epistemology* (Matthias Steup, John Turri and Ernest Sosa, eds.) (2014, 2nd edition), Blackwell.

For a more detailed discussion of the incompatibility of closure with other epistemic principles, see J. Comesaña, *Being Rational and Being Right* (2020), Oxford University Press. Michael Huemer rejects closure on the basis of a similar incompatibility in "The Problem of Defeasible Justification", *Erkenntnis* 54 (2001), pp. 375–397, and so do Sharon and Spectre in "Evidence and the Openness of Knowledge", *Philosophical Studies* 174 (2017), pp. 1001–1037. For a reply to this last paper, see J. Comesaña, "On Sharon and Spectre's Argument Against Closure", *Philosophical Studies* 174 (2017), pp. 1039–1046. Vogel rejects the entailment principle in "$E \wedge -H$," in Dylan Dodd and Elias Zardini (eds.), *Skepticism and Perceptual Justification* (2014), Oxford University Press. For further discussion of this issue, see the exchange between James Pryor and Juan Comesaña in *Contemporary Debates in Epistemology* (cited earlier).

For an encyclopedic introduction to contextualism in epistemology, see Patrick Rysiew, "Epistemic Contextualism", in Edward N. Zalta (ed.), *The Stanford Encyclopedia of Philosophy* (Spring 2021 edition), https://plato.stanford.edu/archives/spr2021/entries/contextualism-epistemology/.

For Dretske's mule case, see Fred Dretske, "Epistemic Operators", *Journal of Philosophy* 67 (1970), pp. 1007–1023.

For Sosa's safety condition, see, for example, Ernest Sosa, "How to Defeat Opposition to Moore", *Philosophical Perspectives* 13 (1999), pp. 141–153. For the Halloween case, see J. Comesaña, "Unsafe Knowledge", *Synthese* 146 (2005), pp. 395–404.

For subjunctive conditionals and their use in epistemology, see J. Comesaña, "Knowledge and Subjunctive Conditionals", *Philosophy Compass* 2(6) (2007), pp. 781–791.

Nozick's theory of knowledge is presented in his *Philosophical Explanations* (1981), Harvard University Press.

6

PYRRHONIAN SKEPTICISM

INTRODUCTION

The skeptic about induction believes that induction cannot justify us in believing anything, and the Cartesian skeptic believes that we are not justified in believing any proposition about the external world. Those two kinds of skepticism are limited, because they think that there may well be some propositions that we are justified in believing. The Cartesian skeptic grants that we are justified in believing propositions about our own minds. The skeptic about induction may, in addition, grant that there is such a thing as non-inferential justification, and also inferential justification when the inference in question can be modelled with a deductive argument (and where the premises of those arguments are themselves noninductively justified). Moreover, both the Cartesian skeptic and the skeptic about induction believe in their own positions, as we reported in the first sentence of this paragraph. From the point of view of Pyrrhonian skepticism, all of these concessions that they make are unwarranted. Pyrrhonian skepticism is universal in scope: it is the thesis that suspension of judgment is the only attitude that is justified with respect to *any* proposition. Thus, whereas the Cartesian skeptic *believes* that we are not justified in believing any proposition about the external world, the Pyrrhonian *suspends judgment* in that proposition, and whereas the skeptic about induction *believes* that induction cannot justify us, the Pyrrhonian *suspends judgment* in that proposition. From the point of view of Pyrrhonian skepticism, the proclamations of more circumspect skeptics amount to a kind of "negative dogmatism." The dogmatists, for the Pyrrhonian, are those who

DOI: 10.4324/9781003208440-9

claim that we can have justification and knowledge. The right reaction to such dogmatism is not, according to them, to claim that we cannot have justification and knowledge—this is what, for the Pyrrhonian, amounts to negative dogmatism. Rather, the right reaction to dogmatism is universal suspension of judgment—which includes suspending judgment on whether suspending judgment is justified.

IS PYRRHONIAN SKEPTICISM SELF-REFUTING?

That aspect of Pyrrhonian skepticism raises an immediate question: is the position self-refuting? A position (or view or claim or proposition) is self-refuting when it entails its own falsehood. For example, the claim "all generalisations are false," being itself a generaliaation, is self-refuting—at least on a literal and perhaps superficial interpretation of what the sentence says. Is Pyrrhonism self-refuting in this sense? Does it entail its own falsehood? It does not. The Pyrrhonian thesis is

> **The Pyrrhonian thesis**: suspension of judgment is the only justified attitude with respect to any proposition.

That thesis does not entail its own negation. Now, one may think that problems nevertheless arise when the thesis is applied to itself. The application of the Pyrrhonian thesis to itself is

> **The Pyrrhonian thesis self-applied[1]**: suspension of judgment is the only justified attitude with respect to the Pyrrhonian thesis.

The conjunction of the Pyrrhonian thesis with its self-application still does not entail that the Pyrrhonian thesis is false. So, again, Pyrrhonian skepticism is not self-refuting. Notice too that the Pyrrhonian thesis entails not only its self-application but also an infinite hierarchy of self-applications—beginning with the thesis that suspension of judgment is the only justified attitude with respect to the Pyrrhonian thesis self-applied:

Pyrrhonian thesis self-applied[2]: suspension of judgment is the only justified attitude with respect to the Pyrrhonian thesis self-applied[1].

Pyrrhonian thesis self-applied[3]: suspension of judgment is the only justified attitude with respect to the Pyrrhonian thesis self-applied[2].

Etc.

This infinite set of sentences is also consistent, in the sense that they do not entail the falsehood of any of the sentences in the set.

Now, if we assume that whenever someone asserts a proposition they are committed (perhaps implicitly) to being justified in believing it, then Pyrrhonian skepticism is in trouble. The Pyrrhonian skeptic asserts that suspension of judgment is the only justified attitude with respect to any proposition. From our assumption, it follows then that the Pyrrhonian skeptic is committed to being justified in believing the Pyrrhonian thesis. But, of course, that is in direct contradiction with the Pyrrhonian thesis self-applied. Therefore, even though Pyrrhonian skepticism by itself is not self-refuting, it is self-refuting when we add to it the assumption that whoever asserts something is committed to being justified in believing it.

But the self-refutation of the conjunction of Pyrrhonian skepticism with the assumption just mentioned does not represent any problem for Pyrrhonian skepticism, for the Pyrrhonian skeptic does not believe that assumption, but rather suspends judgment with respect to it. Someone who accepts that assumption cannot be a consistent Pyrrhonian skeptic, but neither can someone who accepts any assumption whatsoever, and so the inconsistency of Pyrrhonian skepticism with that assumption does not seem to create any special problem. We conclude that it is not at all clear, then, that Pyrrhonian skepticism is self-refuting—although, as we shall soon see, it may well be self-undermining, in the sense that it is impossible to rationally believe in it.

THE INFINITE REGRESS ARGUMENT

The fact that Pyrrhonian skepticism is not self-refuting is not an argument for the position: all sorts of crazy positions are not self-refuting. For instance, the view that the Moon is made of cheese is not self-refuting, but of course we do not count that as a serious reason to believe that it is true. Is there anything positive to be said in favor of Pyrrhonian skepticism? Notice that what we are asking is not whether Pyrrhonian skeptics themselves have a good argument that would convince them that their position is true. Given that Pyrrhonian skeptics suspend judgment on every proposition, they cannot be convinced (of anything) by an argument because such a conviction presupposes that one believes the premises of that argument. But it is possible for there to be good arguments for Pyrrhonian skepticism even if the Pyrrhonian skeptics themselves cannot be convinced by such arguments. It is true that if some argument for Pyrrhonian skepticism were to convince us, then we would face a problem: the argument will be rationally convincing only to the extent that we are justified in believing its premises, but its conclusion assures us that we are not. In this sense, then, Pyrrhonian skepticism is indeed self-undermining, in that it is impossible to rationally convince oneself of its truth on the basis of an argument without thereby losing that rational conviction. It may be for that reason that historical Pyrrhonian skeptics have tended to downplay the rationality of the arguments in its favor, opting rather for the causal efficacy of some considerations which gave them their sought-after tranquility (*ataraxia*). This attitude is not itself free from problems, however, because for a rational subject (as the Pyrrhonians evidently were) the causal efficacy in the removal of belief cannot be completely divorced from justification.

Be that as it may, we can concentrate on those considerations used by Ancient Pyrrhonian skeptics to see if we can extract from them some good arguments in favor of Pyrrhonian skepticism. If we do find a good argument and we cannot refute it, we will then start worrying about the self-undermining nature of our position.

One thing that tended to take away the tranquility of ancient Pyrrhonians was the fact that in philosophy and science (there were no big distinctions between these disciplines back then) there were apparently untreatable disagreements between different theories. The Pyrrhonians would then appeal to the "three modes of Agrippa" to recover the tranquility that the disagreements had robbed them of. Those three modes are the mode of hypothesis (or unfounded assertion), the mode of circularity, and the mode of regression to infinity. The way in which Pyrrhonian skeptics deployed those modes was the following. When a dogmatist asserted a proposition p_1, the Pyrrhonian would then ask for its justification. The dogmatist had then two options: silence or some assertion. If the dogmatist simply remained silent, then the Pyrrhonian would appeal to the mode of hypothesis and conclude that the original assertion was not justified. If the dogmatist asserted some proposition p_2 as an answer, then either p_2 was identical to p_1 or it was a different proposition. If p_2 and p_1 were the same proposition, the Pyrrhonian appealed to the mode of circularity and concluded that p_1 had not been successfully justified. If p_2 was different from p_1, then the Pyrrhonian asked for the justification of p_2. And now the dogmatist has three possible answers: silence, repetition of some proposition already asserted (in this case, either p_2 or p_1), or the assertion of a third proposition p_3, different from the previous two. The first two answers would have run against the modes of hypothesis and circularity, respectively, and, faced with the third option (that of asserting a proposition different from all the ones asserted up to that point), the Pyrrhonian will ask once again for its justification, and the dogmatist will have the same options as before. The dogmatist will not be able to offer different propositions forever (this is the mode of regression to infinity), and so Pyrrhonian skeptics will end up invoking either the mode of hypothesis or the mode of circularity, and will thus recover their tranquility.

This deployment of the modes of Agrippa on the part of the Pyrrhonian can be presented in the form of an argument. In that argument, we will employ the distinction, already explained, between inferentially and non-inferentially (or basically) justified beliefs. We will also appeal to the idea of an *inferential chain*, by which we mean a set of beliefs each of whose members is justified (if at all) by at least one other member of the set. The argument is the following:

INFERENTIAL REGRESS ARGUMENT

1. If a belief is justified, then either it is inferentially justified or it is basically justified.
2. There are no basically justified beliefs.
   Therefore,
3. If a belief is justified, then it is part of an inferential chain.
4. Any inferential chain is such that a) it contains an infinite number of members or b) it contains circles or c) it contains unjustified beliefs.

5. No belief is justified in virtue of belonging to an infinite inferential chain.
6. No belief is justified in virtue of belonging to a circular inferential chain.
7. No belief is justified in virtue of belonging to an inferential
chain that has unjustified beliefs.
Therefore,
8. No belief is justified.

To get from 8 to the official Pyrrhonian thesis (according to which
suspension of judgment is the only justified attitude with respect to
any proposition), we would have to add that if neither belief nor
disbelief in p is justified, then we are justified in suspending judgment with respect to p. Given that disbelief is simply belief in the
negation of a proposition, step 8 already gets us to the Pyrrhonian
thesis.

The argument receives its name from premise 5. Its general structure is that of an argument by elimination: premises 1 and 4 together
entail that there are only four ways in which a belief can be justified,
and premises 2, 5, 6, and 7 eliminate those four possibilities. Many
of the positions in contemporary epistemology can be presented as
reactions to the Infinite Regress Argument, and that is what we will
do in the remaining of this book.

THE REJECTION OF PREMISE 2: FOUNDATIONALISM

Foundationalists reject premise 2, and hold that there are basically
justified beliefs—that is to say, beliefs that are non-inferentially justified. The metaphor commonly associated with Foundationalism is
that of a pyramid, for the idea is that basic beliefs form the foundation on which the rest of our beliefs are based.

But the idea of the mode of hypothesis used by the Pyrrhonians
is that a belief can only be justified by other beliefs, and so for the
Pyrrhonian to say that a belief is not inferentially justified is equivalent to saying that it is not justified at all. How do Foundationalists
reply to this objection? The answer starts by denying the assumption
that a belief can only be justified by another belief. On the contrary, Foundationalists think that experiences can also be a source
of justification—and, at least for empirical beliefs, are actually the

basic source of justification, whereas inferences can only transmit justification. We already discussed the idea of experiences justifying beliefs in Chapter 2, but now we will take a closer look at it.

THE ROLE OF EXPERIENCE IN JUSTIFICATION

Joseph looks outside his windows and sees a green tree. Nothing strange is going on in this situation, and all non-skeptical views will say that Joseph can therefore come to know and be justified in believing that there is a tree outside his window. But how exactly does this justification take place? In particular, what would a Foundationalist say about how this justification takes place?

There are at least three different answers to that question that have been historically important and that also mark theoretically useful distinctions. What is perhaps the most straightforward answer is that the perception of the tree involves the subject, the tree, the act of perception, and nothing else, as represented in the following picture:

Direct Realism: The perception of an external object involves only a subject and the object perceived.

This view has been called "Direct Realism," but also "Naïve Realism," and this latter name indicates that some philosophers have thought the view cannot adequately handle some issues. One immediate worry has to do with the fact that we can *mis*perceive as

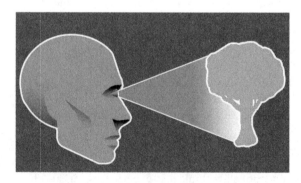

Figure 6.1 Direct Realism (All figures courtesy of Ben Lawrence)

well as perceive. Thus, for instance, we can be subject to some very powerful optical (as well as auditory) illusions, where we see things as having properties that they do not actually have. Moreover, we can also undergo perceptual hallucinations, where there is nothing that we perceive, but our internal mental state is exactly what it would be like if we were actually perceiving, say, a tree. The argument for Cartesian skepticism we examined in the previous chapter trades exactly on the possibility of global hallucination: the hypotheses that we are brains in a vat or inside The Matrix are hypotheses according to which our internal states are exactly what they would be like if we were perceiving external objects but there are no such external objects to be perceived. Direct Realists may have answers to these concerns, but they have been powerful enough that philosophers who have otherwise very different views have rejected the position on their basis.

A view that goes back at least to Aristotle, and that can be seen as being motivated by the objections to Direct Realism just mentioned, has been called "Representative Realism." The idea is that, in addition to the subject, the external object, and the act of perception, there is a fourth element to perception which is an internal object. This internal object is the direct object of experience, and that experience is successful and constitutes a perception of the corresponding external object if and because that external object is connected in the right way to the internal object by the act of perception. There is then an external tree, but also an internal, mental tree, and a successful perception takes place when the direct object of perception (the internal, mental tree) bears the right relationship to the indirect object of perception (the external, physical tree). Illusions are then explained by Representative Realism in terms of differences between the internal and the external object. Thus, when a stick submerged in water looks bent despite being straight, the Representative Realist explanation is that the internal stick really is bent, whereas the external stick really is straight. Hallucinations happen when there is no external object corresponding to the internal one.

On the original, Aristotelian version of Representative Realism, in a successful perception, the internal object is a kind of "copy" of the external object, and they have corresponding properties. Internal and external objects cannot, of course, have all the same properties—the external tree takes up space, for instance, whereas the internal one does not. However, the idea is that we can discern in the internal, mental object, properties that correspond more or less faithfully to properties of the external object. Thus, for instance, small external trees correspond to "small" internal trees, whereas large external trees correspond to "large" internal trees—the scare quotes are needed because of what we just pointed out: that mental objects do not really occupy space. And if the external object is of a certain color, say green, then the internal object will be green as well. The following picture is a schematic version of representative realism:

> **Representative Realism**: the perception of an external object involves a subject, the external object perceived, and an internal object which represents the external one.

Figure 6.2 incorporates the idea just discussed that the internal object is a faithful copy of the external object, so that if the internal object is green (or has the mental counterpart of the property of being green), that is because the external object is also green. But some Representative Realists think that some of the properties of the internal object represent real properties of the external object, but some of them do not. Thus, John Locke argued that because the very same external object can give rise to a green internal object in one subject but to (say) a red internal object in another, color

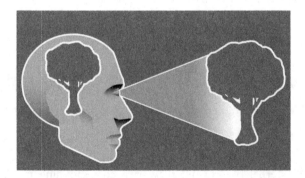

Figure 6.2 Representative Realism

itself is not a property of the external object but is rather a side effect of the interaction of the subject with the external object. The same goes for other properties such as the temperature of an object. According to Locke, because the same liquid can appear warm to a cold hand and cold to a warm hand, in itself it is neither cold nor warm. The properties which do not inhere in external objects but only in internal ones are sometimes called "secondary qualities," whereas the properties that can be possessed by external objects are called "primary qualities." This distinction is certainly older than Locke, as evidenced by this fragment from Democritus, a Greek philosopher who straddled the fourth and third century BCE:

> By convention sweet and by convention bitter, by convention hot, by convention cold, by convention color; but in reality atoms and void.

Which properties belong to which side of the primary/secondary quality distinction varies slightly from philosopher to philosopher, but roughly speaking the idea is that position in space and time, as well as shape, size, and mass, are primary qualities, whereas colors, tastes, sounds, and smells are secondary qualities.

Figure 6.2, therefore, does not faithfully represent the position of someone who is a Representative Realist about perception but

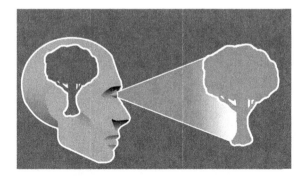

Figure 6.3 Representative Realism incorporating the primary quality versus secondary quality distinction

who also adheres to the distinction between primary and secondary qualities. For them, the picture in Figure 6.3 is better.

Bishop Berkeley thought that Locke's arguments for the conclusion that external objects lacked secondary qualities were good, but he also thought that very similar arguments showed that external objects lacked primary qualities as well. Take, for instance, shape, which is a primary quality according to Locke. Just as the same external object can be perceived as green by one subject and as red by another, the same external object can also be perceived as round by one subject but oval by another. Therefore, if that sort of perceptual discrepancy establishes that secondary qualities are not possessed by external objects, then the same sort of perceptual discrepancy can establish that primary qualities are not possessed by external objects. But the distinction between primary and secondary qualities is exhaustive: every property is either primary or secondary. Therefore, Berkeley concluded, if there were any external objects, they would have no properties whatsoever. But the idea of an object without properties does not make sense. Therefore, according to Berkeley, there are no external material objects, but only internal, mental ones. Berkeley's famous dictum, "to be is to be perceived," is meant to capture this idea that, being mental, these objects only exist as long as they are perceived (and maybe a little bit more, just in case one turns around suddenly, according to a joke by Wimpi—an Uruguayan comedian from the early twentieth century). This position is sometimes known as "Idealism," because

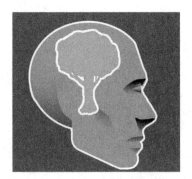

Figure 6.4 Idealism

a popular name for the internal mental objects during the modern era was "ideas" (later replaced by the more serious-sounding but hardly more explanatory "representations"). According to an Idealist, then, what we would normally consider a perception of an external object is nothing more than the presence of an idea in the subject's mind.

At this point, the third figure in the group of philosophers known as the "British Empiricists" comes in: David Hume (Locke was English, Berkeley Irish, and Hume Scottish). This is the same Hume that we already know from the argument for skepticism about induction. He thought that Berkeley's idealism was correct as far as it went, but that it did not go far enough. According to Hume, not only are external objects fictions created by philosophers but so too are philosophers themselves (and any other subjects). There are only ideas, currents of thoughts that sometimes organise themselves in a more or less coherent fashion, and there is a strong temptation to call some of those coherent currents of thoughts a self, but this is an illusion that must be resisted (although if Hume is right, then there is no one who needs to resist that temptation). The ideas are not "had" by a subject, but rather are free-floating. Thus, Hume would represent the perceptual situation we are imagining as in Figure 6.5.

Many philosophers have been convinced by the argument that Direct Realism cannot handle the problem of error or misrepresentation, and have for this reason concluded that something like Representative Realism must be correct. However, certainly not many philosophers would follow the path from Locke to Berkeley

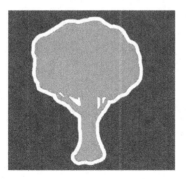

Figure 6.5 Idea of a tree without subject

to Hume and end up accepting that there are only ideas, not subjects or external objects. But according to Thomas Reid (another Scottish philosopher), the problem lies not with the transitions from Locke's Representative Realism to Berkeley's Idealism or from Berkeley's Idealism to Hume's eliminativism about subjects, but rather with Locke's starting point. From Reid's point of view, Hume's position is the inevitable outcome of the introduction of ideas (internal objects) in the picture. In order to avoid the absurdity of Hume's position, then, Reid opts for Direct Realism, eschewing the introduction of intermediaries in perception. Any direct realist like Reid, however, would have to contend with the arguments against that position which we just mentioned.

Here is a picture representing the five positions examined in this section—labelled by the most prominent philosopher associated with the view:

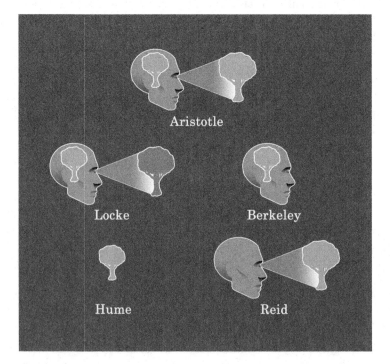

Figure 6.6 Theories of perception

THREE KINDS OF FOUNDATIONALISM

Representative Realists must answer the following question: what is the content of the beliefs that are directly justified by experience—the basic beliefs? Representative Realists have an option here: they can hold that what is directly justified by experience are propositions about ideas, or they can hold that they are propositions about the external objects themselves. Classical Foundationalists opt for the first option: according to them, our experiences directly justify beliefs about our ideas, and we are justified in believing propositions about external objects only indirectly, through an inference which starts from those basic beliefs:

Classical Foundationalism: experiences justify beliefs about the subject's mental life.

Descartes, for instance, exemplifies this kind of Classical Foundationalism. For Descartes himself, the connection between basic and inferentially justified beliefs had to take the form of a deductive argument, and required as an additional premise the existence of God and His omni-benevolence. Other Classical Foundationalists allow nondeductive inferences. For instance, some of them think that we are justified in believing in the external world because its existence is the best explanation of our experiences (a better explanation, for example, than the explanation which appeals to the hypothesis that we are brains in a vat). Thus, we can distinguish between Classical Deductive Foundationalism and Classical Inductive Foundationalism.

Moderate Foundationalists, on the other hand, think that our experiences justify us in directly believing some propositions about the external world:

Moderate Foundationalism: experiences can directly justify beliefs about the external world.

Thus, according to them our experience as of a tree in front of us can justify us in believing that there is a tree in front of us, without the need for any mediating belief about our own experience.

Direct Realists are bound to be Moderate Foundationalists, but an Indirect Realist can also be a Moderate Foundationalist. That is to say, one can consistently hold a position according to which perception involves internal objects mediating between the subject and the external world, but where an experience provides direct justification for beliefs about the external world, without the need for an intermediate belief about the internal object. We therefore have two kinds of classical Foundationalism—deductive and inductive—as well as Moderate Foundationalism.

Which reasons could be given for preferring one form of Foundationalism over the other? Undoubtedly, the alleged infallibility of beliefs about our own ideas was a historically important motive in the adoption of Classical Foundationalism. Thus, Descartes thought that our beliefs about our own mental life give us a certain foundation, and those certainties can be extended by deduction. But at least part of what motivated the transition from classical to moderate forms of Foundationalism is the suspicion that Descartes was not right regarding the infallibility of our beliefs about our own mental life. For instance, it is not obvious that we can always be right with respect to whether what we are feeling is a weak kind of pain or a strong kind of itch. Another historically important source of doubt about our infallibility regarding our own mental life was Behaviorism, which held that which mental states we are in is a matter of which outwardly observable behavior we are disposed to display when subject to certain stimuli. Behaviorism itself fell out of favor both in psychology and in philosophy. But the general idea that our mental states need not be wholly determined by what is going on "inside" of us, but also partly by how some of those internal states are connected to external circumstances, remains alive and well in contemporary descendants of Behaviorism. These descendants include the different varieties of Functionalism in the philosophy of mind. Those Functionalist views can also offer arguments against the infallibility of our beliefs about our own mental lives, and therefore also against classical Foundationalism.

THE REJECTION OF PREMISE 6: COHERENTISM

Coherentists reject premise 6 of the Infinite Regress Argument, but also reject some of the implicit assumptions of the argument. One of them is the assumption that the relation of epistemic justification is asymmetric: that is to say, that if *p* justifies *q*, then *q* cannot justify *p*. Another is the idea that belief is the fundamental unit of justification. Coherentists believe, on the contrary, that a whole belief system is the basic unit of justification, and that individual beliefs count as justified only in a derivative sense, in virtue of belonging to a justified system of beliefs. Thus, Coherentists reply to the Infinite Regress Argument by holding that it is possible for a system of beliefs to be justified in virtue of the fact that its members support each other, without the circularity involved in this being vicious.

One of the fundamental objections with which Coherentists must deal has to do with the role of experience in empirical justification. If, as the Coherentist believes, the justification of a system of beliefs is entirely a matter of the relationships between its members, then there is no place for experience to justify anything. But that is extremely implausible. Let us consider a simple system of beliefs, whose members strongly support each other. Let us suppose that one of the central beliefs in that system is the belief that the subject is at the beach. The other beliefs support, and are supported by, that central belief: for instance, the system also contains the belief that there is sand all around, that the ocean is making certain sounds, etc. Now, if this system of beliefs is justified, then it is justified no matter which subject has it. For instance, John is in fact at the beach and has that system of beliefs. Juliet is not at the beach, but in her house, but also has that system of beliefs. Coherentism has the consequence that both John and Juliet are equally justified, but there is an obvious difference between them: whereas John's beliefs are supported not only by each other but also by John's experiences, Juliet's beliefs are completely disconnected from her experiences.

Coherentists could respond to this objection by holding that we should expand our conception of the system with which our beliefs must fit so as to encompass the experiences of subjects as well as their other beliefs. Thus, John's beliefs are justified because they cohere not only with his other beliefs but with his experiences as well, whereas Juliet's beliefs are not justified because although they cohere with her other beliefs they do not cohere with her experiences. This does save Coherentism from one of the most serious objections that can be levelled against it, but at the cost of its no longer being a position clearly distinct from Foundationalism. Foundationalists too are free to think that the justification of beliefs depends on how well they "cohere" with one another as well as with experience. The difference between Coherentism and Foundationalism would then be reduced to a dispute about whether the justification relation must be asymmetric. Once experience is given a crucial role to play in the justification of empirical beliefs, however, a crucial asymmetry is already accepted, for the experiences themselves are not the kinds of things which can be justified, and so if it is accepted that they can justify then that amounts to accepting a foundational and asymmetric source of justification.

THE REJECTION OF PREMISE 5: INFINITISM

Infinitism is the thesis that infinite inferential chains can justify their members, against what premise 5 of the Infinite Regress Argument says. This option is the one that has received the least attention in the literature, for it seems to face obvious problems. For instance, it would seem that, even if we accept that infinite inferential chains can generate justification, given that we are finite beings, it is not obvious what relevance that can have for us. In response to this observation, Infinitists would surely say that we have to distinguish explicit from implicit beliefs, and whereas it could be true that we do not have an infinite number of explicit beliefs, it is not obvious that we do not have that many implicit beliefs. What is an implicit belief? There are different views about that, but one example is the following: we believe only implicitly that there are no dinosaurs in this room (or, at the very least, we believed it implicitly until we mentioned the proposition in question).

But the Infinitist must answer a more fundamental objection: how can justification be generated simply by the addition of more beliefs? That is to say, it would seem that inference can only transfer justification, in the sense that to be justified in believing that p on the basis of q it is necessary to first be justified in believing that q. If this is so, then Infinitism is false, for it requires that inferences generate justification.

The Infinitist could reply by arguing that justification is essentially a dialectical activity—that is to say, that to justify a belief is to answer objections to it from challenges. Every belief is subject to challenge, and if so challenged then it must be justified. This justificatory activity will inevitably take the form of another belief which supports the challenged one. If and when this further belief is challenged, then yet a third belief must be adduced. Justification is generated by the mere addition of belief insofar as any challenge to those further beliefs can be answered. Thus, the activity of justifying beliefs is, according to this possible defense of Infinitism, open-ended: it continues as long as the beliefs the subject puts forward are challenged.

But this dialectical conception of justification is far from being problem-free. Many epistemologists would argue that we must distinguish between the justificatory status of a proposition for a subject and that subject's dialectical ability to defend her beliefs. A belief may well be justified for Joe even if Joe would not be able to successfully defend that belief from challenges. There are, as always, things the Infinitist could say in reply to this worry, but at this point we move on.

THE REJECTION OF PREMISE 7: POSITISM

Yet another response to the Infinite Regress Argument is that there are beliefs that, despite not being justified, can however generate justification in other beliefs. Thus, this kind of Positism would agree with Infinitism in that inferences can generate justification in addition to transmitting it. This position also has obvious points of contact with Foundationalism, for it also holds that some beliefs play a foundational role—the difference being that whereas for the Foundationalist the foundational beliefs are justified by experience, for the Positist they are not justified at all.

We already considered a kind of Positism in our discussion of the possible answers to Cartesian skepticism, the position according to which we can accept that we are not brains in a vat despite not being justified in believing it.

A serious objection to Positism is that it transforms a doxastic necessity—the necessity of believing that we are not brains in a vat, for instance, in order to be justified in believing almost any other thing—into a supposed virtue. Given that the justification of many of our beliefs depends in a more or less obvious way on our rejection of skeptical scenarios, Positists hold that such a rejection need not be justified to be able to justify. The Pyrrhonian skeptic will not be very impressed by this maneuver.

HYBRID VIEWS

The setup of the Infinite Regress Argument encourages the thought that Foundationalism, Coherentism, and Infinitism are exclusive options, in the sense that adopting one of them precludes adopting another. But some epistemologists have argued that the positions can be combined. A salient possibility here is to combine Foundationalism and Coherentism. For instance, a possible view is that the justification of some beliefs can ultimately be traced to experience, whereas the justification of other beliefs is due to the explanatory relations it bears to other beliefs in the same system. This would amount to holding that Foundationalism is true for some beliefs, whereas Coherentism is true for some others—and this view can be further expanded, of course, by holding that Infinitism is true of yet a third set of beliefs.

The views just mentioned would adopt a "divide and conquer" strategy as a response to the Infinite Regress Argument. But it is also possible to combine views in a deeper way. For instance, according to Foundationalism justification flows only in one direction, from experience to basic beliefs, and from basic beliefs to inferentially justified ones. According to Coherentism, on the other hand, justification is multidirectional, flowing from one belief to multiple others, and possibly flowing back from some of those to the original belief. A possible view combines Foundationalism and Coherentism by saying that some beliefs can only be justified if they bear *both* the right unidirectional relationship to experience and the right multidirectional relation to the other beliefs in the system of which they are a part.

SUMMARY

In this chapter, we examined the most radical form of skepticism, Pyrrhonian skepticism. According to this position, belief is never justified, because the only justified attitude with respect to any proposition whatsoever is suspension of judgment. We started by examining the question whether Pyrrhonian skepticism is self-refuting. We concluded that it is not inconsistent, in the sense that no contradiction follows from the view that suspension of judgment is the only justified attitude with respect to any proposition. It is nevertheless true that Pyrrhonian skepticism is self-undermining in the sense that if it is true then it is not possible to be justified in believing that it is true, and it is not possible either to believe it on the basis of other justified beliefs. Nevertheless, there is an ancient argument for Pyrrhonian skepticism, the Infinite Regress Argument, which is well worth examining.

The Infinite Regress Argument starts from the premises that beliefs must be justified by other beliefs, and that circular or infinite "justifications" are not genuine justifications. Each one of these assumptions has been rejected by epistemologists. Positists reject the idea that all beliefs must be justified; Foundationalists reject the idea that only beliefs can justify beliefs; Coherentists reject the idea that justification is unidirectional; and Infinitists reject the idea that infinite justifications are impossible. Certainly a major part of the importance of the Infinite Regress Argument in epistemology is how different answers to it represent different ways to conceive of the structure of knowledge and justification.

FURTHER READING

For a detailed overview of both Cartesian and Pyrrhonian skepticism, see Juan Comesaña and Peter Klein, "Skepticism", in Edward N. Zalta (ed.), *The Stanford Encyclopedia of Philosophy* (Winter 2019 edition), https://plato.stanford.edu/archives/win2019/entries/skepticism/.

For Ancient Skepticism, see Katja Vogt, "Ancient Skepticism", in Edward N. Zalta (ed.), *The Stanford Encyclopedia of Philosophy* (Summer 2021 edition), https://plato.stanford.edu/archives/sum2021/entries/skepticism-ancient/.

For defenses of Coherentism, see W. V. Quine and J. S. Ullian, *The Web of Belief* (1970), Random House; and Laurence BonJour, "Can Empirical Knowledge Have a Foundation?", *American Philosophical Quarterly* 15 (1978) and his *The Structure of Empirical Knowledge* (1989), Harvard University Press.

For defenses of Infinitism, see Scott Aikin, *Epistemology and the Regress Problem* (2011), Routledge; and Peter Klein, "Human Knowledge and the Infinite Regress of Reasons", *Philosophical Perspectives* 13 (1999).

In *Evidence and Inquiry* (1993), Blackwell, Susan Haack defends a combination of Foundationalism and Coherentism which she calls "Foundherentism".

Views in the vicinity of Positism can be found in Ludwig Wittgenstein, *On Certainty* (Denis Paul and G. E. M. Anscombe, Trans.) (1969), Basil Blackwell, and in José Ortega y Gasset, *Ideas y creencias* (1940), Espasa Calpe. We take the name from James Van Cleve, "Why Coherence is not Enough: A Defense of Moderate Foundationalism", in Steup, Turri and Sosa (eds.), *Contemporary Debates in Epistemology* (2014 2nd edition), Wiley Blackwell.

CONCLUSION

What should you believe? The question is important for at least two reasons: first, we are a curious species, and so we want to know the truth about what interests us; second, we have to act, and we would prefer to act intelligently—that is to say, we would like to act knowing what the possible consequences of our actions are. Because we value knowledge intrinsically and instrumentally, we ask ourselves what to believe. The skeptic about a given topic holds that we should not believe anything on that topic. If the skeptic is right, both our curiosity about that topic as well as the possibility of intelligent action based on our opinions is closed off to us. So, skepticism is important because it represents a possible answer (albeit a purely negative one) to the important question of what we should believe.

Our main objective in this book has been to introduce the tools that you need to understand and assess skepticism about three overlapping subject-matters: induction, the external world, and everything. Because the skeptical arguments presuppose concepts, distinctions, and techniques of traditional epistemology, we also sought to introduce that material in an accessible manner.

It is worth noting that we have left many questions open: How is Gettier's problem solved?; Which theory of justification is closer to the truth, Evidentialism or Reliabilism?; Does it make sense to attempt to define knowledge?; What is the best solution to the problem of induction?; Do we know that we are not brains in a vat?; If we do, how?; What structure does justification have: Foundationalist, Coherentist, Infinitist, or Positist?; etc. In many of these cases, we have left the question open not just out of a pedagogical

DOI: 10.4324/9781003208440-10

motive but also because we ourselves are not sure what the answer is. On this, at least, many philosophers agree: there is no consensus about the best answer for the fundamental philosophical problems. In part that is a consequence of a terminological decision: as soon as consensus is reached regarding how to go about answering a question, the question ceases to be counted as philosophical (if it was so counted to begin with). That happened long ago with the question about the ultimate nature of physical reality, which went from being a philosophical question to a question of physics (in spite of which there still are, of course, interesting philosophical questions about the nature of reality, and also interesting philosophical questions in the foundations of Physics itself), and also more recently when the philosophy of language gave rise to linguistics. But the fundamental philosophical problems, which include the mind–body problem, the problem of free will, and (especially relevant for us) the problem of skepticism, resist consensual solutions for a non-terminological reason as well: they are very hard. This is not unrelated to our previous point: part of the reason why those problems are hard is, precisely, the lack of consensus on how to go about dealing with them. Our objective in this book has been to give the interested reader some tools to approach the philosophical issues surrounding skepticism and to understand why they are so hard.

GLOSSARY

A posteriori: a proposition is a posteriori if and only if it must be justified by relying on sense experience.

A priori: a proposition is a priori if and only if it can be justified without relying on sense experience.

Accessibilism: to say that a factor is internal to a subject is to say that it is accessible in a special way by that subject. Some accessibilist believe, for instance, that a subject's experiences and beliefs (among other mental states) are accessible in that special way.

Analytic conception of philosophy: the task of the philosopher is to provide analyses of interesting philosophical concepts, and the result of a successful analysis is an analytic proposition.

Analytic proposition: a proposition is analytic if and only if it is true solely in virtue of the meaning of the concepts that compose it. The very existence of analytic propositions is controversial, but setting controversies aside an example would be the proposition *All pediatricians are doctors*. (Propositions that are false in virtue of the meaning of the terms that compose it are sometimes called "contradictions." In some other contexts, the term contradiction is reserved for propositions that are logically guaranteed to be false.)

Anti-Intellectualism (about knowledge by ability): to know how to do X (e.g., play a musical instrument) is not to have propositional knowledge about how to do X.

Argument: an argument is a set of propositions, one of which (the conclusion) is supported by the others (the premises).

Associated conditional: the conditional associated with an argument whose premises are $P_1, P_2, \ldots, P_n$, and whose conclusion is C is the material conditional $(P_1 \text{ and } P_2 \text{ and } \ldots \text{ and } P_n) \supset C$.

Causal theory of knowledge: S knows that p if and only if 1. S believes that p; 2. p is true; 3. S's belief that p is caused by the fact that p.

Classical Foundationalism: experiences justify beliefs about the subject's mental life.

Closure principle (alternative): if S is justified in believing p, and p implies q (and S knows this), then S is justified in believing q.

Closure principle (naive version): if S is justified in believing p, and p logically implies q, then S is justified in believing q.

Closure principle for justification: if S is justified in believing p, and p implies q, and S deduces q from p and accepts q as a result of that deduction, then S is justified in believing q.

Contradiction: a proposition that cannot possibly be true, or, equivalently, that is false in every possible world.

Deductively valid argument: an argument is deductively valid if and only if its premises logically entail its conclusion—i.e., if and only if it is impossible for its premises to be true and its conclusion false.

Defeasibility of justification: a subject can be justified in believing a proposition and lose that justification by acquiring more information.

Direct knowledge: we have direct knowledge of a person, place, or thing just in case we have been in contact with that person, place, or thing.

Direct Realism: the perception of an external object involves only a subject and the object perceived.

Epistemic versus practical justification for beliefs: the practical justification of a belief has to do with the consequences of believing, whereas its epistemic justification does not.

Evidentialism: a doxastic attitude of a subject is propositionally justified if and only if it fits the evidence the subject has.

Externalism: not all the factors which justify a proposition for a subject must be internal to that subject. For instance, reliabilists think that the reliability of the belief-forming process is a factor relevant to the justification of a proposition, but whether the process is reliable is not a matter internal to the subject.

Inductive argument: an argument is inductive if and only if its premises support its conclusion but they do not entail it.

Infallibilism about justification: it is not possible to be justified in believing a false proposition.

Inferential versus non-inferential justification: a belief is inferentially justified if and only if its justification depends on the justification of other beliefs; otherwise, if a belief is justified but not on the basis of other justified beliefs, then it is non-inferentially justified.

Intellectualism (about knowledge by ability):   to know how to do X is to have propositional knowledge about how to do X.

Internalism: all the factors which justify a proposition for a subject must be internal to that subject.

Knowledge by ability: we know how to do X when we have the ability to do X.

Logical entailment: a proposition p logically entails (or implies) another proposition q if and only if it is impossible for p to be true and q false at the same time.

Material conditional: a material conditional, $p \supset q$, is true if and only if either p is false or q is true.

Mentalism: to say that a factor is internal to a subject is to say that it is a mental state of that subject. Paradigmatic mental states include experiences and beliefs.

Mentalism (about evidence): the evidence a subject S has is constituted by S's mental states, such as (some of) S's beliefs and S's experiences.

Mere Lemmas Principle: if S is justified in believing p on the basis of evidence e, then p itself can justify S in believing some other proposition q (perhaps implied by p) only if e justifies S in believing q.

Mode of presentation of a proposition: a mode of presentation of a proposition is a way of thinking about that proposition. A single proposition can have multiple modes of presentation.

Moderate Foundationalism: experiences can directly justify beliefs about the external world.

Necessary truth: a proposition is necessarily true if and only if it is true in all possible worlds.

No false lemmas theory of knowledge: S knows that p if and only if 1. p is true; 2. S believes that p; 3. S is justified in believing that p; 4. S's belief that p is not based on any falsehood.

Nozick's theory of knowledge: S knows that p if and only if 1. S believes that p; 2. p is true; 3. if p were false, S would not believe it; 4. if p were true, S would still believe it even if things were slightly different.

Prima facie versus ultima facie justification: a subject is *prima facie* justified in believing a proposition just in case he or she has some reasons for believing it. A subject is *ultima facie* justified in believing a proposition just in case he or she has enough *prima facie* justification for believing it and this *prima facie* justification is not defeated.

Principle of ampliative justification: it is possible for a subject S to be justified in believing a proposition p on the basis of evidence e even if S does not have independent justification for believing some other proposition q such that e and q together entail p.

Principle of Entailment: if p entails q, then no subject S can justifiably reject p on the basis of q.

Principle of justification transmission: if e justifies S in believing p and p implies q and S deduces q from p and accepts q as a result of that deduction, then e justifies S in believing q.

Proposition: the meaning (or content) of those sentences which can be true or false.

Propositional versus doxastic justification: to have propositional justification for believing a proposition one must have sufficient reasons in favor of that proposition, whether one believes it or not. A belief in a proposition is doxastically justified just in case it is properly based on whatever propositionally justifies it.

Propositionalism (about evidence):   the evidence a subject S has is constituted by propositions which are the contents of S's mental states, such as the content of (some of) S's beliefs and experiences.

Reliabilism: S is justified in believing that p if and only if EITHER S's belief that p is formed by a belief-independent belief-forming process, and that process is reliable; OR S's belief that p is formed by a belief-dependent process that is conditionally reliable, and S is justified in believing each of the propositions on which the process depends.

Reliabilist theory of knowledge: S knows that p if and only if 1. S believes that p; 2. p is true; 3. S's belief that p was produced by a reliable belief-forming process.

Representative Realism: the perception of an external object involves a subject, the external object perceived, and an internal object which represents the external one.

Sentence: a sentence is a chain of expressions of a language, grammatically correct and complete.

Skeptical scenarios: a *skeptical scenario* with respect to a proposition p and a subject S is a possible situation where a) S does not know that p, but b) S cannot distinguish that situation from a normal one.

Sosa's safety condition: S knows that p only if, if S believed that p (perhaps in slightly different conditions), p would still be true.

Synthetic proposition: a proposition is synthetic if and only if it is not analytic.

The tripartite conception of knowledge: S knows that p if and only if 1. p is true; 2. S believes that p; 3. S is justified in believing that p.

Truth-bearer: a truth-bearer is something that can be true or false.

INDEX

Taylor & Francis eBooks

www.taylorfrancis.com

A single destination for eBooks from Taylor & Francis
with increased functionality and an improved user
experience to meet the needs of our customers.

90,000+ eBooks of award-winning academic content in
Humanities, Social Science, Science, Technology, Engineering,
and Medical written by a global network of editors and authors.

TAYLOR & FRANCIS EBOOKS OFFERS:

A streamlined
experience for
our library
customers

A single point
of discovery
for all of our
eBook content

Improved
search and
discovery of
content at both
book and
chapter level

REQUEST A FREE TRIAL
support@taylorfrancis.com

Printed in the United States
by Baker & Taylor Publisher Services